COPING WITH LONELINESS

Other Coping books by Dr. Paul J. Gelinas available through The Rosen Publishing Group, Inc.

Coping with Anger
Coping with Your Emotions
Coping with Weight Problems
Coping with Sex Problems
Coping with Shyness
Coping with Your Fears

COPING WITH LONELINESS

By
PAUL J. GELINAS

THE ROSEN PUBLISHING GROUP, INC.
NEW YORK, N.Y. 10010

Published in 1984, 1989 by The Rosen Publishing Group, Inc.
29 East 21st Street, New York, NY 10010

Copyright 1984, 1989 by Paul J. Gelinas

Revised Edition 1989

Library of Congress Cataloging in Publication Data

Gelinas, Paul J.
  Coping with loneliness.
  Includes index.

  1. Loneliness   I. Title
BF575.L7G45   1984   158'.2   83-26460
ISBN 0-8239-0995-6

Manufactured in the United State of America

About the Author

Dr. Paul J. Gelinas is a psychoanalyst in private practice, a clinical member of the New York State Psychological Association, and an accredited member of the American Association of Marriage and Family Therapists and the American Association of Sex Therapists. He is listed in *Who's Who in the East* and various other biographical directories, including the *National Register of Health Providers in Psychology*. The author of twenty published books, he has taught psychology at four universities. His home town, Setauket, L.I., New York, has bestowed recognition by naming a high school for him.

Contents

Part 1

THE PROBLEM

We are all so much together
but we are all dying of loneliness.

—Albert Schweitzer

CHAPTER I

The Prevalence of Loneliness

With the surge of waves breaking on the beach, you walk alone with your thoughts as a pallid moon spangles the water. Loneliness creeps in, slithering silently into your being: memories of lost causes, lost love, lost opportunities. Within you there is a bittersweet entanglement with the past, full of tender regrets, enveloping you in a melancholy that will not let you go. That kind of loneliness is the lot at one time or other of all sensitive human beings. It is almost taken for granted in spite of the sadness of our solitude.

The loves of yesteryear are dormant or dead. Some whom we adored are gone and we remain with our little world wounded but somehow strangely enriched by the pain associated with that kind of loneliness.

But we are particularly concerned here with a common and malignant form of loneliness, that which is perpetuated through unwise action, compulsive thoughts and habits, and self-defeating behavior that so painfully alienates one from others and the world. The person is alone, discouraged because he feels an intruder, casting a negative shadow before him. Unfortunately, others fulfill the lonely person's prophecy of rejection. And in fact who wants to associate with a nervous bore whose opinion of himself is characterized by timidity and shyness, yet who projects a touch-me-not attitude because he seems to avoid fun, spontaneity, and frankness in human relationships?

Psychologists and psychiatrists have proposed various causes and cures for loneliness. Often one is at odds with others in the social sciences, perhaps each influenced by his own specialty or inclinations, his basic philosophy of human relationships. It must not be forgotten that over two hundred systems of psychotherapy have been enunciated, each claiming to allay emotional disorders, including loneliness and depression. One distinguished sociologist has listed four types of loneliness:

Interpersonal—Some widows, as well as others who live alone without friends or with few social contacts, may withdraw within themselves into a state of perpetual loneliness. Some prisoners, likewise shut away from the world, feel detached, rejected, alienated from the rest of mankind. A patient in a hospital may similarly be overwhelmed by a sense of being neglected, forgotten, no longer a part of the wider realm of everyday activities and dreams.

Cosmic—The lonely people in this category have little faith in ultimate reality, no belief in God or in the concept of a power greater than mankind. If man is the sole measure of all things, such persons are hard pressed to explain their own existence. In fact, the person suffering from cosmic loneliness may finally realize that it is as difficult to say there is no God as to assume that such a higher force does exist. Each view is based on faith, regardless of negative or positive assumption.

Cultural—This form of loneliness often afflicts people who have been transplanted to an unfamiliar environment. Immigrants, without friends, unable to speak English, may suffer a cultural loneliness that bears heavily on their ability to withstand the new frustrations.

Have you ever walked in a city where you are a total stranger? Everybody seems hurrying to some destination or goal. You hear their conversation, their laughter. You are in the midst of thousands. No one cares. People seem to look right through you as if you were a mere shadow or were not there at all. Perhaps there is no greater loneliness than that one feels in a teeming city where one is indeed a stranger: the bustle is everywhere, but you are completely alone.

Social—There are those who feel like outcasts, rejected because of their color, creed, or place of origin. Black people may feel angry because of the loneliness created by the nonacceptance of others who are dominated by prejudice. The more angry and rejected a minority group feels, the greater the tendency to unreasonable behavior and violence. Thus is reinforced the original prejudice against the minority, and the resentment deepens on both sides.

Persons of any race, religion, or socioeconomic status may also feel social loneliness. Living "on the wrong side of the tracks" may prevent social interaction with those who are better off financially even though snobbery is denied. Cliques in school or the workplace exclude many, further spreading loneliness. Some resort to the drug scene to escape the sense of rejection. After all, what alcoholic wants to associate with a teetotaller? One seems to say, "Join the gang, get high, or keep the hell out." Another group may qualify for belonging through snobbery, good fellowship, new fun, drinks, drugs, sex. The college-bound crowd whose families have no financial problems, the ambitious boy or girl who is busy earning tuition, each tends to be in his or her own social nook. And many can testify that professors and teachers are not beyond favoring certain cliques at the expense and the loneliness of those they reject.

Indeed, loneliness is a spiritual affliction rampant in our society. It affects both young and old, both rich and poor. Perhaps to be lonely is part of human nature when one is denied the necessities and emotions for well-being and happiness. Most people accordingly are prepared to be lonely, but not to the extent of pain so severe that it envelops them in despair. At that point, the person may stop reacting, the hurt having cut too deep into the very recesses of the soul.

Popular opinion holds that the elderly tend to be the most lonely. To the contrary, a survey made by the University of Nebraska showed that older people are the least lonely in our society. The study revealed that students are the loneliest, followed by divorced parents, single mothers, persons never married, and housewives.

Loneliness has replaced sex as the number one topic on college campuses. Women, particularly in suburbia, also find themselves caught up in the national epidemic of loneliness. The disease—or rather the symptom—is spreading in every stratum of society.

One can actually die of loneliness. Researchers have discovered that social isolation can contribute to heart disease and early death. Dr. William Castelli, a leading authority on heart disorders, has said, "Significantly, the individual who has few social contacts has an elevated risk of heart diseases." Another researcher, Dr. S. Leonard Syme, who has completed two studies on the effects of loneliness, has stated, "Surprisingly, loneliness and social isolation can trigger heart diseases, cancer, and other life-threatening sickness. This is the overwhelming conclusion of at least five well-documented studies."

The extreme loneliness felt by certain people can make them criminally violent; it can even damage the brain, according to some psychiatrists. Dr. William T. McKinney, Jr., associate professor of psychiatry at the University of Wisconsin Primate Laboratory, reports: "We reared rhesus monkeys in total isolation for the first six months of life. From the time they were born, they had no contact with other monkeys or with humans. Such animals when released from isolation were severely disturbed. They huddled alone in a corner, rocking back and forth. They refused to play or associate with others. Furthermore, they tried to hurt themselves by actually biting their own bodies, or they tried to attack large, powerful males. This antisocial behavior, withdrawal, and irrational aggression are just what we see in psychotic humans."

Loneliness, not drugs, is at the core of every young person's problem, according to the director of the Teen-Age Listening Post, in Washington, D.C. Mrs. Alice G. Miller receives numerous calls and visits daily from seriously troubled youngsters. They talk on a myriad subjects, including heroin, pregnancy, and suicide. And in nearly every case, says Mrs. Miller, most of the difficulties are traced to one root—loneliness.

Many people simply don't know where to turn for help. Few will listen or care. Young and old in all groups are sad victims of loneliness. The complaint is generally the same: no one to talk to, no one who knows how they feel, no one with whom to establish deep relationships.

Dr. Phillip Shaver, associate professor at New York University, circulated a loneliness questionnaire that was answered by 22,000 people. It was found that the vast majority—people of all ages from preteens to octogenarians—were lonely.

Lonely people can certainly understand the feelings of the seventy-two-year-old widower who remained all day in his apartment listening to thieves trying the locks on his door. "It doesn't matter to me," he said, "whether I live or not. It's not that much pleasure any more."

Or the old woman who stayed in her bathrobe because "I couldn't think of any reason to get dressed and put on makeup."

The novelist Thomas Wolfe has described loneliness as "a huge, dark wall" that presses from all sides, imprisoning with no escape.

Varied are the suggestions for overcoming loneliness. Get out and do something, the psychiatrists urge, forgetting that the lonely person finds it difficult and at times almost impossible to seek out new endeavors. Join a club, get into politics, go see a movie, get a cat or a dog, they say. And these experts assert that a person who is best able to recover from loneliness is flexible, independent, interested in a number of things, optimistic, and humble. Obviously, a person with those characteristics would not be lonely in the first place. It is like telling a nonswimmer who is drowning that he would be able to save himself if only he could swim.

It is little comfort to the victim of a suicidal tendency to discover that his physician has the same problem. Specifically, doctors in the United States are committing suicide at two or three times the rate of the general population, according to a report by the American Medical Association.

In recent years, dating bureaus—including computer dating—have flourished to serve lonely souls. These agencies assert that a steady diet of sex and television is not enough. All you have to do is to pay their dues and real love will be your reward. Perhaps equally futile are the singles bars, known in the vernacular as "meat markets." The sad fact is that loneliness is catching, and impersonal and mechanical ways of seeking to lessen loneliness rarely work. Another "authority" urges, "Tell yourself that you are grown up, that you can handle your own problem. Don't be afraid anymore—and watch the loneliness fade away."

If these recommendations were effective, there would be fewer victims of loneliness. Unfortunately, failing to understand the basic nature of the problem, the advisers are deceptive, and their remedies actually exacerbate rather than resolve the problem.

If the popular healers are having their day in modern times, they had their prototypes in the past. Feeling lonely? Try boiling a ram's head and eating the brain. That's only one of the remedies recommended by doctors years ago.

In the late 1700's, Dr. Benjamin Rush invented the "tranquilizing chair." Lonely people were strapped into it and spun around rapidly. The idea was to lower the pulse rate and relax the muscles. Another of the doctor's contraptions was the gyrator, a board extended from a hub on which the patient was strapped and whirled around at a dizzying speed. The treatment was supposed to force healing blood to the brain.

Although Quakers were less inclined to use violent methods to treat emotional difficulties—including chronic loneliness— nevertheless they dropped patients through a trapdoor into icy water, or even threatened to kill them in an attempt to terrorize them out of their emotional disturbance.

Many other devices were used in the early nineteenth century, including applying the lungs of a ram to the forehead, putting a spider in a nutshell to be worn as an amulet, sprinkling the shaved head with water lilies, apply leeches behind the ears, and coating the teeth with the earwax of a dog.

If the assorted advice and treatments of today do not assuage your loneliness, you could fall back on the remedies of former centuries. They might prove as effective as some of those given by modern psychiatrists, not to mention the quacks who prey on the multitude of lonely and discouraged people.

Our aim in this book is not to offer worthless suggestions such as using your willpower, forcing yourself to join clubs or churches, falling in love, or petting your dog or cat. Paradoxically, we are not even concerned with loneliness itself. It is our contention, in fact, that loneliness is not a primary emotional disturbance. It is not a disease, but merely a symptom of a deeper personality disorder. Just as pain signifies some physical malfunction within the body, so loneliness signifies that there is something wrong with the personality and the behavior resulting therefrom.

Loneliness seems to say, "Some elements of your personality are somehow out of gear or in disequilibrium." Loneliness is therefore merely a warning signal that there is something radically out of line within the self.

To treat loneliness as a simple entity is like placing a bandage over a wound. The lesion itself must first be sterilized and treated. In other words, in order to overcome loneliness permanently, we must get at the cause or causes of the discomfort, eliminate the basic trouble, and bring about changes in the personality.

How is this to be accomplished? What is the basis for this scientific and proven method of changing the personality and indirectly evoking the conditions for the elimination of loneliness?

It must be noted that the cause of all emotional disorders—except perhaps psychosis—is frustration, the denial of what is needed for a healthy mental condition. Numerous studies, research projects, and experiments both with humans and animals have offered uncontested evidence that psychological frustrations can result in all sorts of mental dysfunctions.

Indeed, if any of the psychological needs are unmet consistently, we can have a variety of emotional troubles, including loneliness.

In contrast, no one is ever pathologically lonely who feels accepted by his peers, has friends, and engages in activities that give him a sense of worth and satisfaction—who is without persistent guilt or fear, and has a satisfactory sex and love life.

The secret of how to get rid of loneliness will be discussed fully in the chapters to follow. The step-by-step procedures will be presented and elaborated in Part 2.

In the process, you will be introduced to and will learn to utilize a system of applied psychology by which excessive loneliness can be eliminated from your life. This formula has been developed over the years by the author in treating character disorders such as chronic loneliness.

It will become evident that loneliness is largely the result of inability to communicate and to interact with others in a manner that strengthens one's individuality.

Although a strong sense of identity enables us to withstand and even to invite solitude at times, it is also true that a person must ultimately depend on others to maintain a feeling of self-appreciation.

We have been taught by history and biology that our self-preservation lies in cooperation with others. Too much loneliness is therefore evidence that we have lost our way psychologically in dealing with fellow human beings.

Meanwhile, let us learn more about the nature of loneliness and the various channels through which it can project itself at the expense of one's comfort. After all, understanding is one of the psychological needs that are necessary for peace of mind and the enrichment of the personality.

CHAPTER II

Anxiety and Loneliness

Anxiety is a state of tension, nervousness, and a general feeling of apprehension. Behind this generalized uneasiness lies the absence of things or conditions vital to our psychological well-being. Somehow, life has denied us the mental health that is felt as necessary for a reasonable amount of happiness. The good things in our existence have largely passed us by. We are blocked emotionally, seemingly beyond our control. In other words, we are frustrated.

This frustration leads directly to anxiety, and that state of mind holds on tenaciously until such time as the essential needs are met, or satisfied. For example, borrowing from our physical being, suppose you have not eaten for some time. You become more annoyed and restless while your whole body cries out in frustration at your need for food. Similarly, if you are denied a psychological need too long, your nervous system responds with anxiety.

Loneliness then may emerge. The anxiety makes you shy, withdrawn, because the timidity it creates makes you afraid to meet new people, to give vent to your spirit of adventure. The anxiety grips like a vise. Knowing how painful further anxiety can be, you are afraid to do anything that might lead to still more disaster.

Your attempts to protect yourself make you wary of other people. Consequently, they think either that you are snobbish or, conversely, that you are a mousy little person afraid of your own shadow. Wanting so much to be accepted, you nevertheless drive potential friends away, and you are alone, miserable in your wretchedness—you do not belong.

Your yearning to do things that would reflect personal achievement is similarly stifled. Your fear of failure prevents you from venturing into areas where you might be successful. In order to avoid the greater anxiety, you withdraw into your inner self, dreaming impossible dreams. Somehow you will become a great actress, a writer, or an artist admired by everybody, but the anxiety prevents you from doing anything that might possibly materialize some of those dreams. You gaze at a moonlit sky, fantasizing some romantic episode or encounter until a cloud passes across the heavens. The light is out, and your heart bleeds in the loneliness.

If you only knew that deliverance could be at hand, if you knew that your anxiety and loneliness were not the real culprits, that rather something deeper within yourself was at fault, then you might be able to act constructively. The essence of the problem is that some essential psychological needs are being shut out of your life, and you must learn to change your ways and even your personality.

David, twenty-eight, had requested an appointment. He sat, obviously nervous, opposite my desk. "Thank you for seeing me," he said, then remained speechless as his eyes darted about the room as if he feared some hidden enemy. His face had a spiritual quality about it; his eyes were slightly hooded with shyness. He gave the impression of a penitent child, arousing in me a paternal desire to help him.

"Well..." I began as kindly as possible. "Take your time, and tell me why you wanted to consult a psychologist."

He still hesitated, rubbed a hand lightly against his thigh, and cleared his throat. His lips moved only slightly. "It's hard—when or where do I begin?" he asked.

"It's generally a bit difficult, the first interview," I volunteered, trying to reduce the tension.

He paused, "I really have little to tell—well, I don't know. Except—maybe it's because nobody cares for me, particularly women."

"You mean that you find it difficult to make friends?"

He nodded his head. "And men, too."

In succeeding sessions, it was revealed that he was indeed a lonely man. His story unfolded gradually. Sometimes he pleaded in despair, punctuated by anger barely expressed but reflected in tightening lips and clenched fists.

His mother had died when he was five years old. He had been extremely attached to her. More than once, his father had impatiently turned upon him, berating him for making too much noise at play. "Don't you know your mother is very sick; you'll kill her with your racket." The child had almost forgotten the events prior to his mother's death, only to recall them symbolically in dreams.

He had been allowed occasionally to stand at the foot of her bed, with strict instructions from his father not to go any farther. His mother would wave a weak hand, saying, "Davy, boy, your father knows best."

He would gaze, strangely fascinated, at her flushed face, almost angelic with the dark brown hair on the white pillow crowning her head like a halo. His father was jealous of him, he had concluded. There pulsed within the child an acknowledged resentment. Tears came to his eyes. "Mommy, I love you," he had said over his shoulder as he was pushed or pulled out of the room.

Toys and play not interesting him, he had brooded, evolving plans to defeat his father—somehow, he would disobey and triumph. But he kept shouting in frequent temper tantrums, "I want my mommy." The father would lower his newspaper and glower at him, "Do you want to kill your mother?"

One day opportunity had presented itself. The nurse had left the bedroom, and both she and the father were in the kitchen speaking in low tones. As though impelled by an irresistible force, he burst into the room and threw himself on the bed, flinging his arms about his mother and kissing her impulsively on the mouth. He felt the quivering of her lips in soft response. "Please, Mommy—get up, Mommy—get up and play with me again." Slowly she opened her eyes and raised a hand to hold him—but it dropped again helplessly on the blanket, and the tired eyes closed.

"David," his father said, bursting into the room, "get away from your mother."

"No, I won't," David hurled back, his lower lip trembling in anger and rebellion. "She is my mother; you won't keep me from her any longer—I love her." His indignant eyes flashed as he was dragged away, and the nurse closed the bedroom door. He hardly felt the slaps as his father berated him. "You little fool—there's a reason why you can't touch your mother."

David's mother had died that very night.

For a long time, the father's reproachful question haunted him, again and again grating against his nerves: "Do you want to kill your mother?"

As the years passed, consciously he knew that his mother had been on her deathbed with tuberculosis, that his father had meant to protect him from the contagious disease. But insidiously and persistently from a depth that he could not fathom, he suspected that he had killed his mother—and strangely he came to feel that to love a woman was to risk killing her. Behind the delusion was the firm visage of his father who had forbidden him to kiss his mother. Irrational fears and guilt were denied on the conscious level; nevertheless they churned in his subconscious mind. Not only might he destroy women, but as a result of his father's strict moral code, he also feared them. He had never kissed a girl, much less sought sexual imtimacy.

The inner conflicts had spread to encompass all women, and ultimately all his interpersonal relationships. The consequent frustrations and anxieties made him withdraw into himself in unbearable loneliness.

It was obvious that at the root of his loneliness were primarily two unmet needs: he lacked freedom from fear and from guilt. The subconscious influences, the fantasies, irrational as they seemed, nevertheless were the causes of his emotional disorder. They had to be reinterpreted on the adult level, a process that was gradually accompanied by a lessening of anxiety and finally restored him to healthy interpersonal relationships. There was no longer a problem of alienation and loneliness because his need to eliminate fears and guilt had been accomplished.

David, as a young child, suffered the frustration of desire for his mother's attention, which he believed was being denied by his father. The conflict, as he grew older, was relegated out of consciousness, almost forgotten, but still operated deep within him. This unresolved conflict was the direct force behind his anxiety and loneliness.

He was subject to moral anxiety because his conscience kept intruding with the irrational fear that he had been responsible for his mother's death. Moral anxiety is felt as guilt and shame. Actually it is the internal agent of parental authority. It threatens punishment for doing or thinking something that transgresses the wishes or the moral code of the parents. But the person with a guilty conscience cannot escape from the tormenting feeling of guilt because it is a psychic force within himself, an outgrowth of fears of parents.

It is certainly ironic that a virtuous person—like David—experiences more shame and guilt than an unvirtuous individual. The reason for this seeming contradiction is that merely thinking something bad makes the virtuous person feel guilty. A less virtuous person feels less guilty because his conscience is more forgiving; also he is perhaps more apt to satisfy his sexual needs, thereby providing a safety valve for his tension.

In moral anxiety, the danger does not reside in the outside world. There may be little or no danger in the physical environment. It lies within the mind. The person is afraid of the fear always threatening to impinge on his thoughts, even though the situation that originally aroused the fear has long been forgotten. It is as if the person carries on his shoulders his childhood self who still directs his behavior.

The pain engendered by moral anxiety may be so unbearable that the person invites punishment to expiate his guilt, thus finding some measure of relief. People sometimes commit crimes in the hope that they will be apprehended—and usually they are. Law officials are familiar with criminals—some with a high degree of intelligence—who leave obvious clues that lead to their capture. When a crime is widely publicized, there are those who come forward claiming to be the culprit; in such instances the desire to be punished is more bearable than the continuing pain of conscience for past deeds real or imagined.

David punished himself by withdrawing from human relationships, by inflicting upon himself loneliness and a sense of unworthiness. The loneliness thus was subconsciously self-willed: he believed that he deserved his wretchedness.

CHAPTER III

Anger and Loneliness

It has been observed that the basic cause of all emotional disturbances, including loneliness, is frustration. Something is lacking in our lives that makes us anxious. If we are dissatisfied, unfulfilled, denied psychological needs—such as a sense of belonging, a feeling of achievement, comparative freedom from fears and guilt—those unmet needs make us uncomfortable, unhappy, and anxious. It has already been noted that by a circuitous route loneliness can be our lot.

In the process, anger may arise. In loneliness that emotion is compounded by acting destructively instead of in ways that either tend to eliminate it or provide a constructive outlet.

We trace anger to frustration. Without that blocking mechanism and the concomitant anxiety, anger tends to be ephemeral or too mild to cause harm to oneself or to others.

Again, advice to control anger is freely dispensed by some psychologists and psychiatrists, who perhaps have little understanding of the motive power behind anger. Some say that you should control it, as if you could shake it off like dust from your sleeve. Forgive and forget, they urge. Anger is an evil, they claim, which should be cast out. Still others assert that you should express it, not hold it back. Let out your anger. It's good for you to lose your temper occasionally. Perhaps it should occur to these advisers that if their theory of assertiveness and free expression of anger were correct, the healthiest among us would be the criminals who strike out indiscriminately against society, or the patients confined in mental hospitals where anger is so freely expressed.

The proper handling of anger through meeting psychological needs will be described in Part 2. First let us see more specifically how anger leads to loneliness. The connection between anger and loneliness can be readily understood from our own experience. If you are unhappy and deprived of things that you need, it is only natural that you should be irritated and annoyed with your situation. You may become a nag, a destructive gossiper, putting down your friends and acquaintances. You find fault, turn against your parents, your lover. And you become known as a nasty person. People turn against you; you are no fun, a crabby person whose temperament is negative and depressing. You are increasingly avoided, and the more people shun you, the more your anger and bitterness multiply until finally you are alone—a lonely person with few contacts, nursing your hate.

Statistics point to the prevalence of loneliness among Americans. Anger, with its accompanying and resultant loneliness, seems everywhere. It is most noticeable in the abruptness of manner, coldness of demeanor, discourtesy, and general bad temper of people who reflect the basic discontent in their lives.

Dr. Richard J. Gelles of the University of Rhode Island, in a recent survey of 137 families, found that violence of one kind or another plays as large a part as love in the life of the average family. Dr. Susanne K. Steinmetz of the University of Delaware has declared that violence plays a more prominent part in family relationships than love and affection; she reported that 60 percent of the families surveyed indicated that violence was part and parcel of their lives. Older children frequently attacked their parents, causing physical harm or injuries. Pregnant women were the object of physical attack by their husbands, and women beat their husbands as frequently as their husbands assaulted them. This finding contradicted the common belief that only husbands beat their spouses. The fact that the male is frequently the recipient of physical abuse was concealed because of his shame and humiliation at being beaten by a woman.

Anger and violence exist in the mansions of the wealthy as well as in the homes of the poor. This volatile combination respects no social or educational boundaries, since frustrations are prevalent on all socioeconomic and cultural levels.

Anger seems to be an inherited characteristic when severe

hindrances to self-realization occur. But apart from a tendency to react by fighting when one's life is threatened, anger is also more widespread in households where violence exists as an example to be imitated. Violent parents bring up children who follow their emotional instability. The family environment is conducive to hitting and biting between brothers and sisters. These children then carry their destructive ways outside the home, into the school and the street.

In this period when anger seems rife in public places, when young criminals kill and mutilate for thrills, the situation remains largely unchecked because research is in the wrong direction, neglecting the elementary fact that frustration is the cause of anger and of the alienation known as loneliness. This situation is perpetuated by the example of parents.

As the studies reveal, many people feel that anger and violence are normal in domestic life: they know no other way. Is it any wonder that loneliness and a sense of rejection and unworthiness permeate many households?

Stanley, thirty-two, was an angry man. Tall and well built, he appeared self-confident enough, in fact perhaps too much so, which was soon revealed as a protective device against a poor image of himself. As he abruptly took the chair that I offered, he scrutinized my face as though seeking signs of counterirritation on my part.

He had been referred by his physician, who suspected that the man's ulcer was exacerbated by psychological problems. I urged him to tell me about himself, his work, his family—and anything else that came to mind. He flipped a lighter, puffed on his cigarette, and allowed some of the smoke to blow across my desk, which I viewed as a hostile though perhaps unconscious act.

Stretching out long legs, he leaned back. "All right, Doc—cure my ulcer," he challenged.

I explained that a psychologist does not cure any physical ailment, but that a troubled person can prevent the healing process or worsen an existing condition. "You and I in this office work with your mind, with emotions that in turn can have great influence on the body," I added.

He scoffed. "You know, Doc, I think you're full of shit. I don't think anyone can help me."

"Possibly I can't—and of course you don't have to see me unless you want to."

He lowered his eyes. There was a pause. "Okay," he said finally, a bit conciliatorily. "I'm a mess, I'm willing to try anything. But who would have dreamed that I would be forced to see a shrink?"

"Forced?" I questioned.

"All right, let's forget the runaround. What do you want me to do?"

"I don't want you to do any particular thing. Merely be honest with me and with yourself. Drop that facade of yours and tell me just what is your problem—as you understand it. Why did you come to see me?"

He planted his heels squarely on the floor. "Hell, I already told you—I'm sick. Maybe here, too," he added, pointing to his head.

Stanley was one of two sons of a small contractor who carried on the rough tradition and ways of his native rural Italy. Stanley was slow academically, rebelled against the nuns of the parochial school, and dropped out, refusing any further education. His brother, Joe, continued his studies until he was graduated from law school; he passed the bar examinations and gradually built up a lucrative practice.

Meanwhile Stanley drifted, alternatingly surly and devil-may-care in attitude. He fell into the leadership of a street gang, where his strength and bravado made him a hero to his peers. Cheap sex and impulsive fights in alleys or in dimly lit bars seemed for some time to give him the satisfaction necessary for his shaky self-esteem.

But within him grew a great discontent. The loneliness was somewhat dissipated by alcohol and by orgies that nevertheless left him deeply discouraged. On the surface, however, he was calm and cool in the streets or at odd jobs. Even as he beat an opponent ruthlessly, he felt that he was merely defending his turf. He was always loyal and generous to friends or to anyone who recognized his "greatness," allowing him to maintain the facade of an inflated ego. He needed repeated assurance that he was worthy of others' admiration. And even when defeated in his various encounters, he would lick his wounds and concede that the other guy was the better man—until the next time.

Stanley was both good and evil in extreme measures, guided by an angel as he sought in vain for salvation. Alternately he let loose the devil in him because so frequently it was the stronger. He cursed the fate that in the end always left him weak and in despair. The loneliness was ever ready to lacerate his soul.

He wanted to love, but he didn't know how to grasp it nor to make it his own. Handsome in a rugged way, ready with laughter between scowls and curses, he did meet a girl who cared for him deeply. His happiness seemed complete until the demon and the bottle took over. One day after he had beaten her, thrown her against the wall, and heaped curses upon her, she was gone, leaving not even a note. Awakening from a stupor, he wailed in self-pity: women were always ungrateful, the world was rotten, and there was no such thing as love, merely deception and faithlessness.

On one visit to my office, Stanley passed another patient who was leaving. That patient was in sharp contrast to Stanley, who always came in his work clothes. The man wore slacks, jacket, and well-matched tie. Smooth of hair and manners, he reflected care of his person and attire. But Stanley sniffed, "Goddam, what a dandy—I wonder if his mother knows he's out," he commented to the secretary.

"You don't like him?" I said, noting Stanley's unkempt hair.

Stanley took his customary chair. "Bet he's a gay blade," he muttered.

"You don't like well-dressed men. How about women?"

"No way—I think well-dressed broads are fine. I just hate sissies."

"How does your father dress? Your brother?" I asked.

"My brother, Joe—well, that's different. He's a good lawyer. A damned good one. He's got to dress the part."

I suspected that he was protesting too much, particularly as he continued with a spate of praise for his brother. He went on until I interrupted.

"Joe seems to deserve much approval—being your father's favorite because he was so promising and well liked."

"Yes," he said. "Joe was always the right Joe. I never was any good."

"Do you think you were ever jealous of your brother?"

"Hell, no," he retorted. "Joe earned and is well entitled to—well, he's not only smart; he's got a house facing Long Island Sound, two beautiful children, a Lincoln, and also a station wagon. He always got everything—but he always was worthy of what he got. And he used his influence to get me a good job at the nuclear plant here. I could never hope to even come up to his standards. Joe is the right sort."

I detected a slight harshness in his voice when he repeated, "Joe is a good man."

I suspected that the subject needed further consideration, but the session was over, and Stanley left without another word. There had been little progress, and I wondered if his defenses were so firmly set that perhaps I could do little more. He was still the same truculent person, although at times I caught a look in his eyes that was almost childlike, a begging soft look that immediately disappeared. It was often followed by obscenities, criticism of the office decor, or attacks on me, calling me a quack, saying that I charged too much for my services even though he had insurance coverage.

During the next session, he was particularly abusive. "You like your other patients better than me—you hate me, don't you? I'm a fucking cluck and you're a leech sucking the blood of nuts and queers."

"You're angry," I said simply.

He lowered his head, suddenly subdued for a moment. That look, so alien to his usual self, wistfully returned. "Don't mind me, Doc . . ." He hesitated. But later he walked out of the room more slowly. And now alone contemplating the day's work, I told myself that surely there must come a time when we would recognize the nature of his demon, and perhaps even tap his angel for the good that lay so deeply buried in this strange and annoying man.

Not many days afterward, he burst into my office. "I saw a horse!" he exclaimed.

For a moment, I thought he was merely recalling a pleasant childhood experience that in his enthusiasm he wanted to share with me. Then I saw the horror on his face; his lips were white and tightly drawn, his eyes wild, and his right cheek twisted in uncontrolled spasm. It was evident that he was suffering from shock. Mechanically, he sat down and muttered, "I'll be all right—I know you can help me."

After being lulled into a trance, he settled down. Now calm after about half an hour, he said, "What the hell did you do to me? I remember now your telling me to close my eyes and that I would go to sleep." He looked around the room, still a little dazed. Blood had returned to his cheeks. "You hypnotized me, you bastard."

"How do you feel? Tell me about the horse now."

He responded in his usual aggressive manner. "You know," he began, "there is a goddam politician who is riding in a horse-and-buggy—someone told me... Imagine a son-of-a-bitch who uses a horse on the busy highways from Orient Point to Huntington to get votes." He rambled on, "A four-legged—I hate horses. I never want to see a horse again."

I recalled that he had reported a few dreams in which he was frightened by a horse, and I concluded that it symbolized some authority figure in his childhood. But free association about the dreams yielded nothing; it was always readily blocked while his mind leaped to other elements. However, he had never openly expressed any fear of horses. Of course, recalling one of Sigmund Freud's famous cases of a child's fear of a horse, I had withheld any further probing until a more auspicious occasion presented itself. Slowly in succeeding sessions, repressed memories came to Stanley's consciousness, and the story of his phobia finally emerged in full.

Stanley was afraid of anything connected with a horse. He did not know why he had the fear. He only knew that he had had it as far back as he could remember. Psychotherapy uncovered the following:

When Stanley was four years old, his father had brought home two toy horses, white and spangled with gray, one for Stanley and one for Joe, who was a year younger. In a fit of anger, Stanley had broken his brother's toy, for which he had been severely punished and made to give his own horse to Joe.

Analysis revealed that Stanley had been very jealous of his younger brother and secretly wished him dead so that only he would enjoy the devotion and attention of his father. The breaking of Joe's toy signified a destructive act against the brother.

The punishment and the guilt that he felt became inextricably linked with the animal. Thereafter, when he saw a horse or came in contact with one, the fear became as real as it had been in his early childhood. Stanley as an adult was suffering from neurotic anxiety that had turned him into a cruel and angry man, and its origin was masked by an unconscious compulsion to speak only well of his brother. He found himself gradually rejected, alone after he left his gang, a lonely man, bitter and discouraged.

Neurotic anxiety is aroused by a threatened danger, an anticipation that the original frustration will inevitably return. Stanley did not know as a adult that he feared most the rejection of his father; and certainly he did not know, nor did he want to know, that subconsciously he still resented his brother. The device of rationalization—the acceptance of an opposite—deceived him into loving and praising Joe.

Yet his street fights were a taking out on others what his inner self perceived as striking his brother. His opponents were indirect targets of hidden hostility that existed when he was a mere child.

Neurotic anxiety often causes a free-floating apprehension, a fear that something awful will happen. Stanley's nervousness was evident, although covered up by bravado and foul language. Like a person lost in the darkness of a forest, with evil spirits on all sides, Stanley never knew when the fear and loneliness would become unbearable, driving him out of his mind. His anxiety pursued him like hidden and leering shadows in the depths of his neurosis.

With Stanley that fear took the form of a phobia, an emotional disturbance marked by the intensity of the fear, which is out of all proportion to the danger posed by a specific object. To the average person it doesn't make sense to be afraid at the sight of a horse, as was Stanley.

A person afflicted with a phobia is deathly afraid of such objects or situations as insects, elevators, mice, crowds, open places, crossing the street, or any of numerous others. The fear seems groundless, but it triggers extreme anxiety because subconsciously it symbolizes an experience charged in the past as well as in the present with fear, guilt, and anxiety.

Another form of neurotic anxiety may be observed in panic situations. One often reads about a previously peaceful person suddenly going berserk and killing strangers. Afterwards he cannot explain his action; he can only say that he became so tense that he had to do something or he would have exploded.

The panic reaction is the result of long and severe frustrations, anxiety that has been bottled up. Such a person is generally described as quiet and lonely, seemingly harmless in his timidity and shyness. Stanley had not reached that stage, but his readiness to start a fight on a very flimsy pretext displayed some characteristics of a panic reaction.

Weeks later, after working through his problem and the complexities that had dominated his behavior, Stanley was a changed man. It was as if a great weight had been dropped from his shoulders and, symbolically, a cancer had been excised from his soul. He had been burdened with the frustration of being denied the love and affection that he so wanted as a child. He had felt frustration and a smoldering jealousy in thinking that his brother was their father's favorite. The frustration followed its course to anxiety, soon followed by unrelenting anger.

Now I was surprised to see him in a blue striped suit, a subdued but smart tie, shoes shined, hair neatly trimmed. I almost gasped in amazement.

He smiled, controlled and somewhat amused at my obvious consternation. "Don't you think I can dress up, too?" he said.

"I must admit that..."

He cut me short. "I'm not afraid to compete with my

brother anymore—and it might interest you that I have joined my father in his contracting business. The old boy was very happy with my decision—give me a few years and..."

"Come in," I invited him to his usual chair.

"No," he said, still beaming. "I don't need you anymore. This is goodbye."

Before I could respond, he started toward the outer door, then paused. "You know," he said, "I think you're okay." With a wave he left, never to return. At last he had harnessed his angel and his demon into a workable team.

As in this case, it is generally not acknowledged that anger is the indirect cause of loneliness. It is not that people leave you alone because of your personal appearance or your political views. On the contrary, loneliness is actually invited by its victim by unacceptable behavior. The lonely person is basically angry, and his or her behavior projects that inner hostility toward people and the world.

Accordingly, the aim of the lonely person is not directly to get rid of his loneliness, but rather to find the source of the anger that engenders it. Once this has been done, and the unmet needs fulfilled, loneliness will no longer be a problem.

CHAPTER IV

Loneliness and Shyness

A shocking 140 million Americans are plagued by shyness: 70 million are chronically shy, and another 70 million are painfully shy in some situations. This sense of inadequacy, according to Dr. Phillip Zimbari, director of the Stanford University Shyness Clinic, is one of the greatest emotional problems in the country. The effect of shyness is devastating; it robs life of much, makes it a morass of fears, uncertainty, and horror.

Dr. James Hodge, professor of psychiatry at Northeastern Ohio University, has stated that two out of three people suffer from shyness. It is a widespread problem that causes anxiety, loneliness, and emotional turmoil for millions. It creates all sorts of embarrassments and often leads to deeper psychological disorders, to unrelenting loneliness—and sometimes to suicide.

What causes this national ailment? What makes one person shy and another at ease, outgoing, able to meet people with grace and to establish interpersonal relationships with confidence and spontaneity? Who is one person open and fun to be with, readily accepted as a friend, while another withdraws into his corner, afraid to open up, lonely as a dark cloud in a windless sky?

Some psychologists say that shy persons are really selfish, self-centered, thinking that the world should revolve around them, preoccupied with themselves.

It is true that concern for the self is generally uppermost in the mind of the shy person. He wants so much to be loved, admired, and accepted. The fact is that he has been denied fulfillment of his needs more severely than has the person who does not suffer from shyness. Also, the shy person may be more sensitive to slights and deprivations.

The shy person nearly always has a history of being denied the satisfaction of very important psychological needs. Statistics indicate that from 10 to 16 percent of the population will suffer mental illness severe enough to be candidates for a mental institution during their lifetime, and many more will be made unhappy by emotional disturbances. It appears evident that a good number of these people have been neglected and have experienced traumatic situations that have diminished their ability to function adequately.

Shy people are not necessarily mentally ill in the true sense of the term, but they are blocked in their relations with others. It is true that there are more unhappy people than is dreamed of. A study of a group of New York City residents disclosed that about 80 percent were emotionally upset enough at one time or another to warrant psychotherapy.

Regardless of the possibility that shy people are neurotically inclined, it behooves us to recognize their suffering and try to understand the defenses they attempt to erect against their shyness.

The shy person avoids social gatherings, misses recreation and good fellowship. Everywhere people seem happy in comparison with his or her limited existence. The mass media, particularly television, render even more lonely those who are already denied the pedestrian pleasures of ordinary life. The commercials feature radiant men and women, beautiful clothes, lustrous hair softly fluttering in a mild breeze, a glamorous cruise ship or island paradise permeated with romance. The world seems to offer excitement, accentuating the feelings of rejection of those who are alone, too shy even to reach for such delights. It is true that not all shy people are subject to such severe turmoil, but many are in enough misery to warrant pity and understanding.

How does one escape from the wrenching experience of loneliness, the throes of inadequacy? How does one break away from the tightening snare of shyness? Where is the escape?

Many and varied are the choices available, some ultimately replacing shyness with tragedy and wrecked lives.

One of those is bravado and a devil-may-care attitude—the

opposite of the inner feelings. The shy person forces himself to project a facade of bravery, taking chances, driving recklessly, undertaking stunts so dangerous that they suggest suicidal tendencies. The man has to climb a high mountain; the woman cannot be satisfied until she is the greatest among her peers. Unfortunately, the shyness remains lurking behind the screen of their hectic actions.

The goal is never really attained. There is always a higher barrier to overcome that beckons with its excruciating challenge and its promise of exorcising the demon of shyness and loneliness.

There is also, in desperation, the headlong decision to join a fast crowd, regardless of how it may contradict one's own moral code. If one has to choose between staying at home or going with a drinking clique, well, drink you must. And anyway, when drunk the shyness falls away and for a while a false happiness shines through the haze. A case in point follows:

Julia had managed to graduate from a two-year business school near her home in spite of her reticence and shyness. She blushed at any personal remarks and would walk out of the living room if an uncle—who was inclined to drink— offered an off-color joke. "You're pretty as a picture," he would tell her as the redness of her hair seemed to reach her cheeks and neck.

At eighteen she had never had a date, nor was she interested in boys. So she proclaimed while her femininity cried out for expression—denied, but nevertheless racking her being with the pain of frustration.

After several interviews, during which her nervousness betrayed her, she had given up looking for a job. One night, attending a church social with her mother, something happened that changed her life.

She was bored and restless as she watched uninterestedly a slide show given by an elderly man who had recently visited the Holy Land. Feeling slightly faint, she whispered to her mother, then headed for the corridor and the ladies' room. She splashed cold water over her face, but still the faintness persisted. Deciding that fresh air would help, she walked to the end of the corridor and emerged next to the parking lot.

She breathed deeply in the night air, but the pressure in her head did not relent. The great restlessness remained. What could she do to break out of the imprisonment that characterized her life? Something had to happen, she told herself. She knew that she was beautiful in some ways, and yet there emanated from her an aura that drove people away.

As she mused in her discontent, she heard laughter from one of the cars—raucous laughter, but happy laughter. It went through her like a knife and seemed part of her secret yearnings.

"Hi, Julia," someone yelled. She recognized one of the boys, a rowdie, but still popular, who had left school before her graduation. "Come on, have a beer." He waved a can like a flag, unsteady on his feet in the light from the open church door. She almost felt glad he was drunk—not knowing why.

She moved toward the car like an automaton to the blaring radio, hardly aware of the motion of her limbs. In days to follow, she could not recall what went through her mind. She only knew that something strange and stronger than herself impelled her forward.

She seized the can and drank, letting the beer overflow from the corners of her mouth. It was as if a dam had burst, sweeping all in its path. And she laughed, laughed until her sides ached.

Certainly a few cans of beer and the laughter of teenagers are not the road to perdition. Moderate drinking often is a mere social custom. But insignificant as it may seem, that brief interlude in the parking lot had in Julia's case an element of rebellion that originated in long suffering and frustrations almost too hard to bear. She had experienced loneliness without end, and now there was no turning back; in time she became a seemingly hopeless alcoholic, because going to hell was preferable to the loneliness and emptiness.

Every psychologist can cite cases of people who in despair turn to self-destruction because their psychological need for love and affection, companionship and self-worth has been denied. They kill themselves drinking like madmen on the highways, they turn to crime—anything to relieve the boredom, the restlessness that will not let them go. Loneliness, if not alleviated through the satisfaction of basic psychological needs, can wreak havoc. Loneliness can indeed be a killer.

Shyness may seem to originate from several specific factors, even though earlier or current frustration may really be the culprit. For example, a man may be very self-conscious about being comparatively short in height or, on the contrary, too tall. Being different is frequently a cause of discomfort, since the prototype in our culture is often a measure of values and acceptability. Being too fat or too thin is contraindicated, although for women the media have largely made the concept of thinness desirable through the portrayal of skinny fashion models. Fat women, of course, are hurt by the comparison.

But the man who is on the thin side is viewed as a weakling at the mercy of any brawny challenger. The pot-bellied, beer-drinking good Joe peers at his paunch as a sign of masculinity, of good living and independence.

However, the small penis is consciously or unconsciously viewed as a mark of unmasculinity, an appendage that has been shameful ever since the boy hid it as soon as he could escape from the gym shower, while some of his peers ran about dangling their bigger penises as a sure sign of imminent manhood. It is usually of little solace to point out that the man who is embarrassed by his small penis has little to fear in his relations with the opposite sex. The size of the penis has little influence in bringing a woman to orgasm. And whatever the psychological predisposition to favor a larger organ, that idea is soon eliminated when love appears in the relationship. The female is more influenced by psychological factors than by the physical. Affection, consideration, kindness, concern for the woman's welfare all combine to lessen the importance of any physical characteristics.

Strange indeed is the Freudian concept that a man is shy and fearful—guilty—because as a five-year-old child he expected castration by a punitive father if he allowed himself sexual fantasies about his mother.

You feel inferior and shy because you cannot dance and shake your hips as voluptuously as the girl or boy next door. The elderly man feels left out because he cannot skate and play handball as the younger men do: the implications are of manliness and sexual potency, and accordingly, the older man is often envious of the younger. Yet if his potency is the equal of those of younger years, he is called a dirty old man instead of being recognized as a symbol of good health.

One of the greatest fears of many men is to be considered effeminate. Early in childhood he was warned against being a sissie; he must hide his emotions, not cry "like a girl." The man with any tendency toward femininity may spend endless hours denying both to himself and others any characteristics that may be deemed feminine, such as a way of walking, use of the hands in fluttering gestures, and other mannerisms considered of doubtful manliness. Such a person out of fear and shyness may turn into a braggart and a fighter. He is so afraid of femininity that in self-defense he assumes an exaggerated manliness, which actually betrays what he considers a weakness. When a man boasts about hatred of feminine men, it may be indirect evidence that the traits he professes to detest are actually his own. He hates what is within himself, fearing that it will make him an outcast among real men. The man who is sure of his masculinity is not concerned with the sexuality of others, feeling sufficiently strong not to be threatened by ways alien to his own.

Analagous to a man's sense of inferiority and shyness caused by the size of his penis is the problem of some women about their breasts. Their breast size is of great importance because our culture has equated small breasts with lack of sexual attractiveness.

In the minds of many women, this idea is constantly reinforced by the general sexual climate. People laugh when a comedian says that Dolly Parton for years has not been able to see her shoes when standing erect. They laugh because big breasts are sex symbols in the popular mind. *Playboy* magazine and similar periodicals have amassed millions for their owners because men like to look at women's bare breasts. Little wonder that women feel left out if they are less amply proportioned there than in the pornographic images. The plastic surgeon makes as much money transfiguring breasts as he does remolding noses into the Grecian ideal.

There are many other areas that bother people, that make them feel shy and often lonely because they do not fit the norm demanded by the culture. Nevertheless, this zeal for conformity—whether it be more hair on head and chest, a straighter nose, larger breasts or penis—is fundamentally due to deeper frustrations of basic psychological needs. In the end, seeking trends of passing fashion as a means of avoiding shyness or loneliness is like a dog chasing its tail. What will he do with it if he does catch it? What happens when the girl buys the latest styled pair of jeans? It is still herself who is encased therein, still eaten from within because her real needs are unsatisfied. In other words, if her psychological needs for love, affection, self-respect, and freedom from guilt and fear are not met, the surface efforts to solve her inner problems are unavailing.

The formula of defeat has already been articulated. First is the frustration, then anxiety, followed by irritation or anger as a reaction to the anxiety. The next step in this deepening of the problem is guilt: in every shy person there is guilt, either conscious or subconscious.

Here is a point where our feeling of inferiority becomes a real feeling of guilt. We suspect a responsibility for our own shyness and loneliness. We must bear the consequences. It is as if life has passed us by and we must resign ourselves to the unhappiness. That is a state of mind often encountered.

Another source of conflict may lie in the Freudian concept that women are envious of the male because he has a penis and she has none. Penis envy is vehemently derided in the Women's Lib movement, and many other women assert that penis envy is solely in the mind of the chauvinistic male. One might with equal logic say that some men are envious of women because they have breasts, which are denied the male. Whatever the charges and countercharges in this contest between the sexes, the fact remains that some females would prefer to be men, and some men would not be averse to being women.

Leaving out any envy based on philosophical or anatomical differences, considerable evidence indicates that it is not uncommon to find a girl seeking a male self-image. Vice versa, a boy may imagine himself happier by seeing himself nearer the feminine ideal than that of his own sex.

The conflicts and anxieties are worsened when a person confuses the masculine with the feminine side of the personality. The girl may feel it would be advantageous to be a boy. As a male, she would be allowed to do many daring things, join her brother's gang, steal apples, jump fences, and engage in all sorts of activities generally frowned upon for the female sex.

If the reality of current norms, or even false assumptions on the part of others, discourage her to the extent that she feels trapped permanently in being a girl, she may decide that after all she is and must remain a girl. Such an almost inevitable decision may make her feel insecure, inferior, as well as resentful and bitter. Belief in the unfairness of the world becomes encased within her for the rest of her life: all girls are bad; they are inferior and underprivileged.

If such a girl is caught in that conflict between femininity and masculinity, she may screw up her courage to decide, "I will be a boy—believe it or not, I am a boy."

From then on, she may identify herself with the images of boyhood, leading a boy's life in her imagination and later in actions. She talks in her brother's slang, walks like a trooper, throws things around, leaves her room in a mess, and flatly refuses cooking, sewing, doing laundry, or playing with dolls. In short, the negatives associated with boyhood become her own. She is rough, even cruel.

This distorted image is often strong enough to change her into a real tomboy. And physiologists have observed that in such cases the internal glands are sometimes affected to the extent that puberty may be retarded, slowing the development of breasts and hips.

On the contrary, a boy may well conclude that life is too dangerous and demanding for him and that girls have all the advantages. And he decides—especially if he has been dominated by an older brother—that the image of being a girl might be an escape. He becomes a sissie, avoids fighting, proclaims his cowardice a virtue. He cannot bear disharmony in human affairs, and calls his weakness love of peace. (Not that all antiwar activists belong in this category; many believe that international conflicts should be settled without bloodshed.)

The boy who would be a girl seems to develop a sense of beauty, without allowing for patience and deficiencies. Physically, he remains a man, but his sexual potency is often underdeveloped, although he may consider himself highly sexed.

In some cases, we have greater complications. One layer of the personality may be masculine and another layer feminine. The boy may really be a sissie physically and emotionally, but a bully and a tyrant at the same time. Some of the great conquerors in history have belonged in that category. Or the girl can be masculine in self-image, in physique, while emotionally she is actually too feminine. Certainly in these instances we see evidence of two distinct personalities in the same person.

Another device to lessen loneliness engendered by a sense of inadequacy is inverted snobbery, the process of displacing a desired object by its opposite. If you cannot afford a Cadillac, for example, you may declare that you hate big cars. You deceive yourself with inverted snobbery by professing that small cars are more appropriate for intellectually superior people.

The dynamics involved begin with shyness, followed by frustration and anger. To protect yourself from anxiety because you cannot attain a certain goal or object you may use the mechanism of inverted snobbery.

Shyness and loneliness in their devious ways can involve deeper motives, which we often try to hide even from ourselves.

CHAPTER V

Loneliness and Self-Hatred

If anger and guilt fail to find a constructive outlet, or otherwise are not neutralized by satisfaction of the person's needs, ultimately the anger turns inward in the form of self-hatred.

The person seems poisoned by self-generated venom, detesting himself, taking the blame for all his shortcomings. He purposely becomes his own worst enemy, agreeing with those who disdain him, feeling unworthy, and increasingly being rejected both by himself and by others. He withdraws into a seemingly endless loneliness. No one is more lonely than the person who sees his loneliness as warranted, as rightful punishment for deeds real or imagined.

Mankind, in fact all living things from plants to the most sensitive of human beings, are subject to an immutable law of existence. All things must grow—all must die.

Everything and everybody that lives is impelled by a cosmic power to develop, to reach for self-fulfillment. Opposing that force is an irresistible urge to die; to cease to grow, and finally to be annihilated. Death is inescapable, and no organism has ever dodged it. And yet life always follows death. A child is born to replace the parent who has met his own fate. Life and death are like the swing of a pendulum, which generates its own rhythm from birth to death to birth.

In one basic instinct, the impetus to live is created as soon as the sperm meets the egg waiting for impregnation. The dried and seemingly lifeless seed falls from plant or tree and awaits the proper environment to be born again, to be transformed into life once more. But in each case, there was a period of dormancy corresponding to death. This motivating urge to stir into new life can therefore be termed the life instinct. It is the force all around us. It cannot be denied except at our own peril. We are born to grow, to mature into a mold predetermined by a higher insistence.

Everyone has that cosmic and dynamic power to reach for a full life, to reach a level of existence that has already been ordained by his heredity and potentialities. Failing to harness the course of our lives to this universal push and pull results in actually choosing its opposite, which is equally powerful— the death instinct.

This contrary death instinct has only one aim, that of assuring that all living things die. The cycle between life and death must include a period of dormancy, a sort of decay before life begins again.

We struggle against this death instinct by allying ourselves with the life instinct, living to the fullest of our capacity, providing our bodies and minds with the fulfillment of our vital needs, not only for nutrients and shelter, but also those of a psychological nature.

What has this concept of the life instinct and the death instinct to do with self-hatred as opposed to self-worth and happiness?

The answer is simple. The person who hates himself hates life itself. He has allied himself with the death instinct. He is prematurely dying by his own hand. His personality shrivels like a dry and dying seed. It is a lonely existence without hope, as if the core of himself recognizes the course he has chosen and the tragic end already in sight.

If a man or woman can be constructive, that trait unfortunately can be opposed by destructiveness. Each tendency is there. The person with self-hatred has yielded to the force for self-ordained destruction.

Many, therefore, are committing suicide without their own knowledge, some slowly, others plunging into self-annihilation in one fell swoop. The intense restlessness and often the subconscious impulse to escape may be evident in the statistics of automobile accidents. It is well known, of course, that many accidents are not accidents at all, but impulsive and headlong decisions to end an unbearable dilemma.

More Americans have died in accidents on the nation's

streets and highways than on battlefields, according to the National Safety Council. Traffic deaths have accounted for a staggering 1.9 million deaths. The nation's nine major wars killed 648,952, about one-third the number of traffic deaths.

To ascribe all those tragedies to anger and the urge for self-destruction would, of course, be difficult to justify. But certainly many of these unfortunate people were driven to deliberate self-destruction. The victims cannot testify how many were the result of carelessness and neglect. But a large number of the guilty ones were impelled by a subconscious force, daring to play a sort of Russian roulette with their lives, risking recklessly their lives and those of their victims.

We cannot answer the many questions that arise here. It would be equally impossible to interrogate the dead in order to determine how many of the offenders were denied the meeting of their legitimate needs so that they chose in desperation any dangers to escape the emptiness of their lives.

Car wars are breaking out on highways across America. Roads are being turned into bloody battlegrounds as frustrated and angry motorists use tons of speeding metal as deadly weapons. Incidents of cars being used as weapons and acts of personal violence involving motor vehicles have increased about 25 percent in the last five years, reports Captain Joe Lowe of the Irving, Texas, police department.

In Houston, a driver became infuriated because traffic was holding him down. He purposely plowed into the car in front of him at such a speed that the car became airborne and struck another car, killing three people.

Another police official, Capt. John LeVrier of Houston, says, "We have several cases a week in which people become angry, fighting as a result of an accident, and using their cars as a tool of their aggression." Further he says, "We had a man just recently who went on a rampage with his car, and struck deliberately several other vehicles on the street. He went through an apartment complex and hit parked cars there until his own was totally disabled."

Another street skirmish, a simple fender-bending incident, ended in tragedy. The two drivers exchanged words; one got a shotgun out of his car and killed the other.

Detective Thomas W. White, of the Boston Metropolitan Police, added to the recital of frustrated motorists who seek an outlet for their anger on streets and highways. "We've had documented events," he said, "in which as a result of an argument over a traffic accident, people have used their autos to run down other individuals."

When a hothead is behind the wheel, a car is a perfect vehicle with which to blow off steam. Urban life these days is full of frustrations, and a car that can go fast and make a lot of noise is an object with which to express one's frustrations, says Jeffery Z. Rubin, an associate professor of psychology at Tufts University.

Again we see the familiar sequence of frustration, anxiety, and anger. It can be concluded that some of those who acted so illogically in response to anger would, given time for reflection, feel self-hatred.

Personality traits definitely lead, in some instances, to fatal auto accidents. Some people tend to go through life with a chip on the shoulder as a result of chronic frustrations; they are nervous and usually leap before they look. These are the people whose needs have not been met, who feel blocked and stifled in constructive outlets—and hate themselves.

Dr. Chester W. Schmidt made a study of fifty single-car fatal accidents in Baltimore and concluded that "as a group the victims were significantly more belligerent and negative... they reacted poorly to stress." Psychiatrists who reviewed the results of the study concluded that "... victims in single-car accidents had distinct character traits which undoubtedly brought their involvement in their own death."

Dr. John W. Shaffer, a psychologist at Johns Hopkins University School of Medicine, says that the evidence speaks for itself. "There is no doubt," he states, "that significant relationships exist between fatal accidents and the drivers' personality characteristics."

Dr. Jean Rosenbaum, a psychiatrist, says, "If you suffer frequent accidents you could have avoided—even minor accidents like spilling coffee or dropping a lit cigarette—you may be emotionally ill. You may be having those accidents on purpose." She suggests that you ask yourself the following questions: "Do I have more accidents than other people? Do they occur one after another? Do I feel I'm a victim of bad luck?"

If your answers are "yes," you are probably accident-prone. Some people need to attract the attention of others. Having an accident such as falling down or dropping a dish serves that purpose. "People who are lonely and desperate for companionship will often have an accident to get attention," says Dr. Rosenbaum, adding that "some accident-prone people harbor guilt feelings." They feel consciously or subconsciously that they have done something wrong. They become upset and have an accident to punish themselves.

Accident-prone people are unhappy. Sometimes they give the impression that they are calm and light-hearted when actually their inner feelings are the opposite. They are always charged with negative feelings, which work like a magnet attracting accidents. Accident-prone people are starved for love and affection and lack other psychological needs. They must change their entire program to attract happiness instead of negative factors in their environment.

Self-hatred and self-punishment were early evident in the case of Nita, a twenty-three-year-old, dark-haired girl. At one time she must have been very attractive, but when led by her mother into the office the young woman was pale, drawn, and listless.

The mother, obviously dominating and impulsive, sat opposite my desk and talked compulsively, expressing her concern for her daughter's condition. The girl sat almost facing her mother, motionless, with glazed eyes, seemingly not interested in the interview.

Finally, turning from the mother, I sought to draw the daughter in the conversation. "Your name is Nita—do you feel that you need help?"

She stirred and responded almost in a whisper. "Maybe you can help me with a new diet," she said. "I'm too fat."

Her mother broke in, "My God, look at her—she's getting to be a skeleton. And still..."

Indeed the girl was emaciated. "Would you care to tell me if you have any particular problem," I persisted.

"My daughter is mentally ill," the mother blurted. "We've tried everything," she added coldly, then flung at her daughter, "You know you're sick—you're killing yourself."

Nita sat upright in her chair. Her face, previously expressionless, suddenly came to life in animosity. Her fists were clenched, her lips pulled thin from stress and anger.

"I hate you, Mother," she exploded, eyes blazing.

A tirade of accusations poured forth, finally ending with, "If you only knew how much I hate you, Mother."

"Nita," the mother exclaimed, biting off her words. "How could you—stop that, stop it right now! We'll take care of some of those things when we get home."

I was amazed at that point to see the girl seemingly crumble, leaving her like an untended puppet. Deep sobs shook her body, and she lowered her head as if expecting a blow. Finally, with all intensity gone, she said quietly, "Mother— you know—you know that I love you. I do, I do!" Then in a pleading voice, she asked, "May I wait in the car? You can tell the doctor what he needs to know." She slunk out like a chastised child.

The girl gave evidence of a love-hate relationship with her mother. Why did she hate her? Why did she love her? Or did she really mean those penitent words of love? Were they a cover, a defense against the hatred—and why did she feel it necessary to love her mother, if she did do so? Here was an unusual case. A girl close to anorexia nervosa, and two women so enmeshed in contradictions that both seemed lost.

The mother proceeded to tell the story of her daughter, the while revealing much about herself. Nita was an illegitimate child. "She never knew her father, and," the woman added coldly, "neither did I."

I put in, "Does she ever express a desire to know or to see her father?"

"Never," she replied. "He never even existed as far as she was concerned."

It occurred to me that the girl must have repressed the thoughts but that subconsciously she might still be reaching out for the missing paternal figure. I made a mental note to investigate this further with Nita, but the mother now seemed determined to unload her own feelings. I listened without interruption.

Nita soon after birth had been left with her grandparents. Apparently cold, rigid, and bound by duty to do "the Christian thing," they provided a small farm environment, meager clothing, food and shelter. But they apparently convinced the child that she was the unfortunate consequence of a sinful moment, a moral laxness of which Nita became the embodiment.

"But what else could I do," the mother now protested to justify her actions. She continued in a whining voice, tinged with hostility, "I was a waitress, with a job in the city, and anyway, I didn't—I couldn't take care of her." She made a move as if to wipe a tear from her eye—a tear that wasn't there. "It was they who did not want me to get rid of the pregnancy; in their holier-than-thou minds I had committed a mortal sin, and they wanted me to pay for it. So I said if they wanted the baby, let them take care of her."

"Did you ever see Nita during those early years?"

"Once in a blue moon until I got married when she was eight years old." she replied. "Remember, I was hurt. The more boyfriends I had, the more I wanted to forget. Oh, I hated them all. Men are all the same—bastards."

I looked at her, amused.

"Oh, well, you're different—a doctor," she added conciliatorily. "You seem to be a nice man." Pausing to adjust a shoulder strap, she gave me a coquettish look. "You wouldn't take advantage of a weak woman, would you?"

I told myself that she was far from being a weak woman. Basically, I guessed, she was scheming, self-centered, and terribly deceptive in her own defense and self-justification. I was glad that the session was over as I explained that I would work with Nita but that it might be best for her to consult another psychologist if she wanted treatment.

"Oh, I don't need psychotherapy," she tossed over her shoulder as she flounced out, a smile on her lips.

I scolded myself for the countertransference, the feelings of positive dislike for the woman.

Nita's succeeding sessions began a turbulent journey among

the boulders of her defenses. The caverns of her subconsious mind through which we groped wound crazily through the labyrinth of her neurosis, revealing intermingled self-hate, fears, and guilt.

The compulsion against food abated slightly, but she was still rebellious and impelled by forces seemingly outside herself. Yet she gradually became more trustful of me. Sometimes her eyes lighted up with the soft gleam of tentative love. I cherished those moments in which I was becoming the recipient of something she had always feared to give. I had concluded that her greatest need was for love, affection, and meaningful communication.

Nita began to understand the nature of her problems, and how they had affected her life. The mother deeply resented her daughter, whose birth had complicated her existence. She viewed the child as a symbol of man's inhumanity to woman. But with that uncontrolled and often unacknowledged hostility came guilt. The mother sought to expiate her hatred by being overconcerned with the child. The cold domination she rationalized as a protection against the possibility that Nita might make the same mistake she had made. After she married and took Nita to live with her, from time to time in fits of anger she would fling the caustic remark that she wished the child dead, that life would have been better if Nita had never been born. Later she would gush over with assurances, saying, "I'll always keep you—because I love you." Thus plagued with inconsistencies, Nita was always insecure; she feared constantly the possibility of being abandoned—as she had been abandoned at the time of her birth.

A complication emerged that was not at odds with other dynamics of Nita's problems. She found herself erotically attracted by her stepfather, who was considerably younger than his wife. Although no sexual intimacy had occurred, and the man was not even aware of Nita's feelings, the forbidden fantasies evoked terrible conflicts in Nita.

Thinking erotically about the stepfather involved the fear of punishment and abandonment by the mother, the fear that was so traumatic in Nita's childhood. On the other hand, revenge for her mother's cruelty was tempting: what greater blow against her mother than a sexual affair with her stepfather.

Her confusion and ambivalence could not be dissipated. She dreamed awful dreams in which she killed her mother, and awoke bathed in sweat and trembling. Alternately she could not resist the sexual thoughts, which were ever menacing and horrible in their compulsion.

It was then that the course of anorexia nervosa began to emerge. She could not bear the thought of being fat because in her subconscious having a bulging belly was to be pregnant—by her stepfather. The need for love and sexual fulfillment was inextricably linked to guilt. And deeper still was the pathological urge to repeat her mother's role in bringing forth an illegitimate child.

Alongside these conflicts, the thought of putting on weight impinged on the defensive desire to make herself unattractive, unfeminine, as a protection against her sexual thoughts. Making herself skinny would repel her stepfather—in fact, any man—and thus help her to avoid temptation.

However, as Nita seemed to have reached a good deal of self-understanding and begun to satisfy supplementary needs, something happened that plunged the girl into her greatest tragedy.

As her progress became more evident, with more self-responsibility and less dependence on her mother, the older woman suddenly turned to unreasonable hostility. Her daughter was slipping from her.

Deep within her she did not want her daughter to get better. She had taken the girl to the psychologist to soothe her own conscience, to prove to herself that she was indeed concerned with the welfare of her daughter. She had not counted on her own tenacious desire to hold on, to dominate her daughter's life.

Now, as she realized that health and comparative well-being were returning to her daughter, her subconscious hatred of her daughter reared its head again. The woman panicked, feeling that her whole psychological structure was coming apart.

Barging into the office, she flung a check on the desk. "This will settle our account," she announced haughtily. "Nita is getting worse instead of better, while you have been growing fat at my expense. Nita will not be coming anymore." With those words, she left the office and slammed the door.

Indeed, there are more evils in this world than most of us dream of. I thought of poor Nita who had never been allowed to take her life in her own hands. Nita, who almost began to see a new light, was being damned by a mother who preferred in her twisted mind to choose torture rather than happiness for her daughter—a life abandoned to the death instinct.

There is no doubt that loneliness frequently reflects self-hate. The feeling of being inadequate and unattractive—even when entirely undeserved—may become a hindrance because others tend to accept one's self-estimate. That is the price paid for self-deception: a ready-made concept of one's poor self-image.

You have known people who were not too heavily endowed with intelligence or skills, yet who seem to control their world, acting indeed as the captain of their destiny. You may have ascribed their success to luck. However, an aura of self-love and confidence may be largely responsible for their good fortune. On the contrary, self-hate and a poor concept of oneself tend to mark the lives of lonely people who too often exhibit self-defeating behavior.

CHAPTER VI

The Great Cop-out

You can, of course, turn to drugs as a means of escaping loneliness.

If you're to fool around with drugs to meet what you presume to be your needs, you may as well know how to use them, be familiar with some of the esctasies and the dangers connected with them, as well as the sophistication of the swinging crowd. It may be your decision to go to hell by degrees or in sudden oblivion. That is your privilege and your decision.

The ability to speak a common language with your drug dealer may give you a sense of being "with it," a feeling of some gratification—at least until you find yourself in an open doorway with limbs all awry. At that moment you would not give a damn whether you look graceful in rigor mortis. They'll just put a tag on your big toe before sliding you into a morgue compartment.

"All right," you say. "I want to live, to get high, laugh. Would you deny me that? My old man gets high on booze. What's the difference?"

You're right on—no one has the prerogative of leading another person's life. So you're going to make the drug scene. Here is a manual for the drug user. Enjoy yourself—and good luck. You'll need it as you cast your lot with the death instinct.

NARCOTICS

Opium (Papaver somniferum)

This is the dried, coagulated milk of unripe opium poppies. You can get it from your dealer by asking for "opium," "op," "penyan," "hop," or "black stuff." It is dark brown in color, a plasticlike substance.

Opium, as you may have seen in the movies, can be smoked through a long-stemmed pipe. Today, however, it has lost its popularity, replaced by its more powerful derivatives morphine and heroin.

Morphine

An odorless, light brown or white powder, morphine can be obtained from the friendly neighborhood dealer or from a doctor. Morphine comes in tablets, capsules, or powder form. It is widely used by addicts when heroin is not available. Morphine is either taken by mouth or injected as a liquid. It acts on the central nervous system as an analgesic or pain killer, remaining in the body from 6 to 18 hours. It has a variety of names, including "white stuff," "hard stuff," "M," "morpho," "unkie," and "Miss Emma."

Heroin (diacetylmorphine)

This substance is two to ten times more powerful than morphine, although it is a synthetic alkaloid of morphine. Heroin is one of the most popular drugs among addicts. The effect is an intense "high." However, tolerance to its effects increases rapidly. In other words, the longer the addiction, the more one needs in order to duplicate the original highs. At the beginning, you may be satisfied with two to eight mg., but soon you may find yourself needing 450 mg. daily.

The drug is odorless, a white or light brown powder. It is called "H," "junk," "Harry," "horse," "white stuff," "snow," "joy powder," "sugar," or "smack."

The common method of indulgence is intravenous, called mainlining. Heroin is also taken by mouth or inhaled, but both these methods give a slower and less intense reaction than mainlining. Heroin may also be injected under the skin, termed "skin popping."

The effects may continue for as long as ten hours. After that you need another fix, as you feel rocks lacerating your belly and guts. If you have the money, you can quickly seek your savior, the dealer. If you're out of money, you'll be tempted to steal your maiden aunt's gold tooth—anything to stop the torture.

Codeine (methylmorphine)

This drug comes in the form of a crystalline powder or tablets. A weak derivative of opium, it is less addictive than morphine or heroin, and giving up the habit is not as hellish an experience. It may remain in the body for up to 10 hours.

Codeine is taken internally by swallowing a liquid. The street name is "school boy."

STIMULANTS

A variety of stimulants are available on street corners and in other more respectable places such as schools and work-places.

A stimulant acts on the central nervous system. The most widely known stimulant is caffeine, found in coffee, tea, colas, and other drinks in very mild form.

Synthetic stimulants used in more powerful forms are the types covered by drug-abuse laws. Cocaine, for example, is covered by the narcotics laws.

A person under the influence of a stimulant of this type is excessively active, irritable, excitable, and euphoric. His pupils are dilated, and he goes for long periods without eating or sleeping.

Amphetamines

The drugs under this classification have been employed medically for obesity, fatigue, Parkinsonism, and depressive states. However, their unwise utilization for these disorders has frequently resulted in the development of harmful dependency; that is, the patients had inadvertently become addicts.

Psychological dependency creates problem behavior such

as hyperactivity and hallucinations. Continuous use of amphetamines can lead to psychosis. It can also produce high blood pressure and abnormal heart rhythms.

Amphetamines are often used in a social setting. There is also the solitary user. Sometimes the drug is mixed with alcohol—a dangerous concoction.

When injected into a vein, amphetamines become highly addictive, and the obnoxious effects are similar to those experienced with heroin. In fact the excitability caused by intravenous injection may cause greater danger than that connected with heroin. The paranoia that is associated with amphetamine addiction often takes the form of violence, and sometimes even murder.

Amphetamine addicts often stay awake for days, without food, experiencing hallucinations with bouts of paranoia. The drug creates a sudden heightened mental power—at least in the addict's imagination—followed by a tendency to violence and suspicion of being persecuted. As the high state fades, the user falls into a stupor, a long deep sleep.

Methamphetamine (speed)

The use of speed has been increasing at an alarming rate among teenagers and young adults. It is the most potent and dangerous of all the amphetamines. The effects are like those of the other forms, except far more intense.

Speed comes in capsules or tablets and in liquid form for injection. Most speed addicts began with low dosage taken by mouth. Seeking more kick, they increase the dosage to 150 to 250 mg. daily and then take the intravenous route.

The toxicity of the drug varies with different people. One person may need ever increasing dosage to maintain the desired effects. The drug remains in the body detectably for 24 to 36 hours. Under the influence of the high, the user becomes more and more talkative, strung up, excited, and engages in purposeless activities.

The street names for the amphetamines include "bennies," "pep pills," "peaches," "roses," "hearts," "cartwheels," "dexies," "oranges," "footballs," "coast to coast," and "L A turnabouts." These apply to amphetamines in general. Special terms for speed are "meth," "crystal," and "bombida."

Cocaine (Erythroxylon coca)

This drug has come to be widely used. Originally indulged in by a sophisticated, wealthy crowd, it served to smooth socialization among people who deemed themselves superior, daring, devil-may-care, and fashionably rebellious. Today, its use has spread to all socioeconomic levels, despite its high cost.

Cocaine is an odorless white powder obtained from the coca bush. Like the amphetamines, it is prohibited under the narcotics laws.

At one time, cocaine had wide acceptance in the medical profession as an anesthetic; however, it has been replaced by synthetic substitutes known as Procaine and Novocain.

Cocaine is generally sniffed, absorbed through the membrane of the nose. It can also be injected directly in a vein. The resultant fix strongly stimulates the central nervous system. An addict who wants a more intense reaction mixes the cocaine with heroin into a "speed ball." Morphine is similarly used in combination with cocaine.

The user experiences euphoria, feeling full of energy and a sense of superiority. The pupils of the eyes are dilated and fixed. The exhilaration dissipates quickly, to be replaced by tremors and severe anxiety accompanied by depression. This mental state is generally combined with hallucinations and paranoid delusions.

The street names for cocaine include "coke," "snow," "happy dust," "E," "flake," "speedballs," "snowbird," "Cecil," "stardust," and "Bernice gold dust."

DEPRESSANTS

Depressants affect the central nervous system and are used medically to induce sleep and as a mild tranquilizer. However, if one abuses depressants as a chronic crutch, symptoms of alcohol intoxication appear. The user falls asleep during the day. His walk may be staggering or stumbling, giving the appearance of disorientation. The pupils of the eyes are dilated, and the person finds it difficult to concentrate.

Barbiturates

These drugs are sedative or hypnotic. They act on the central nervous system. Physicians prescribe them to calm patients who are under stress or who suffer from insomnia, high blood pressure, epilepsy, and many other physical or psychological ailments.

In a recent year, the Food and Drug Administration reported that one million pounds of barbiturates were available in the United States. Converting this quantity to tablets or capsules would provide 24 doses for each woman, man, and child in the country. It is obvious that there is much abuse of barbiturates both by the medical profession and by lay people who obtain the drugs without prescription.

Like heroin, barbiturates are habit-forming and lead to addiction. A person hooked on these drugs is really hooked. Withdrawal brings about a hellish sequence including convulsions and lack of muscular coordintion similar to epileptic fits. Withdrawal should not be attempted without the supervision of a physician; convulsions can recur up to the 16th day of abstention.

There are three classifications of barbiturates. The phenobarbitals are slow in reaction but of long duration. Examples are Luminal and Eskabarb. Another group are intermediate in starting and duration; they include butabarbital and amobarbital. Examples are Butisol and Amytal. The third group, including secobarbital, and pentobarbital, are short-acting, fast starters. Examples are Seconal and Nembutal.

All these drugs are manufactured in tablets or capsules. They are taken by mouth, intravenously, or rectally. A daily dose of 0.4 gm. produces addiction, depressing the user's mental and physical functioning. The abuser is slow in speech, has chronic constipation, and his judgment is erratic.

The general street terms for the drugs are "goof balls,"

"goofers," and "barbs." More specific names for the several categories are as follows:

1. Pentobarbital sodium—"yellow jackets," "yellows," "nimbys."
2. Amobarbital sodium—"blues," "blue heaven," "blue birds," "blue devils."
3. Secobarbital sodium—"reds," "redbirds," "red devils," "seccy," "pink."
4. Amobarbital and secobarbital—"tuinal," "tuies," "rainbows," "double trouble."

Chloral Hydrate

Like the drugs already discussed, chloral hydrate is addictive. However, habituation to chloral hydrate is less frequent, probably because it severely irritates the gastrointestinal tract. The user is likely to be turned off because of extreme stomach pain and to look elsewhere for his kicks.

Chloral hydrate, generally provided in capsules, looks like gelatin. Heavy doses are required to maintain the desired kick. It can be taken orally or rectally. Withdrawal involves fits of delirium.

The drug mixed with alcohol is called a Mickey Finn. Drinking establishments have been known to slip a Mickey Finn in the beverage of an unruly customer in order to get rid of him. The results are similar to acute barbiturate intoxication: gastric irritations and vomiting. An overdose also produces breathing difficulties and dangerously low blood pressure.

The slang terms for this drug are "a Mickey," "a Peter," and "knockout drops."

HALLUCINOGENS

This class of drugs brings about behavior and mood changes. The user in a trance may recline or sit quietly for hours. But on occasions fear and terror affect him, depending on whether or not the trip turns out to be good or bad. The pupils of the eyes dilate, and blood pressure, heart rate, and blood sugar increase. The user may also suffer nausea, chills, flushes, sweating, irregular breathing, and tremors. There may, in addition, be changes in the senses of sight, smell, and touch, and inability to distinguish the passing of time.

Of course, these descriptions of a bad trip are not the inevitable consequences of using a hallucinogen. It would be ridiculous to say that a few puffs on a marijuana cigarette must result in such extreme reactions.

Marijuana (Cannabis sativa)

Derived from a plant of the hemp family, marijuana grows up to 14 feet in height. Its active ingredient is tetrahydrocannabinol, which comes from the amber-colored resin of the female plant.

The drug was formerly used to relieve pain and induce sleep. Although researchers are still looking for its medical application, there is little encouragement because of marijuana's unpredictable effects. It possesses the dual capability to stimulate and to cause depression.

Marijuana looks like green tobacco, sometimes containing seeds and stems. It is generally hand-rolled in heavy paper. The so-called joint is closed at both ends because of the dryness of the weed; this causes it to be shorter than an ordinary cigarette. When lighted and smoked, the joint smells like a burning piece of rope or alfalfa. The odor hangs in the air, and for a while it can be detected on the breath and clothing of the smoker.

Marijuana is also smoked in a pipe. Sometimes tobacco is mixed with it to slow the burning. Another method is known as steamboating, smoking it through a roll of toilet paper. Still another method of use is extracting the resin and taking it by mouth with tea or mixed in a cookie. The resin can also be extracted by boiling the marijuana plant.

The ritual of smoking in groups is prevalent. One person takes a few puffs, then passes the joint to the next person. The user holds the smoke in his lungs as long as possible to get the most effect. The burnt remnants of the joints, called "roaches," are saved to make another joint.

The effects are similar to those associated with alcohol. The user speaks more freely, with less inhibition, thinking that his remarks are clever and deeply philosophical, although they are frequently childish. However, the overall effects are determined largely by the user's personality, and also by a sharing of sensations with others in the group. After some fifteen minutes, many of the participants begin to feel restless, and time seems to be standing still, distances distorted. Meanings deteriorate and concentration is difficult. Depth and time perception are distorted. Continuing the smoking for some 20 to 25 minutes in large amounts may bring on hallucinations. However, the total trip can last three to five hours.

The aftereffects cannot be readily noticed. There seems to be no physical addiction, but the habit frequently becomes psychologically difficult to break. Withdrawal certainly does not bring about the torments associated with other drugs.

The dangers of the habit have been greatly enhanced by the large-scale introduction of hashish, a concentrated resin from the marijuana plant. The ability to manufacture the ingredients to any desired strength poses dangers of increasing negative possibilities.

Many are the slang terms for this prevalent drug, including "pot," "tea," "grass," "weed," "stuff," "rope," "hay," "joint," "reefer," "hemp," "Mary Jane," "locoweed," "hashish," "Texas tea," "Acapulco gold," "a stick," "goof butt," "jive," "sweet Lucy," "stinkweed," "bhang," and "ganja."

LSD (Lysergic acid diethylamide)

This synthetic drug was developed in 1938 by Dr. Albert Hofman, a scientist at the Sandoz Research Laboratories in Switzerland. But it was not until 1943 that its perception-altering properties were discovered.

The powerful chemical action of LSD is caused by ergot, a fungus that grows on rye, wheat, and other grasses. A single ounce of the drug is powerful enough to provide 300,000 of the usual doses.

The drug was formerly used to treat psychotic patients, but unsatisfactory side effects were so common that this practice has been discontinued. It was found that LSD can cause chromosomal damage resulting in congenital birth defects. One of the many effects upon the user is a sense of complete detachment from reality. Thus, it may lead to serious injury and even death. The addict can become extremely dangerous to others.

LSD is a white powder that cannot be definitely identified except by analytic tests. It is generally taken by mouth in tablet or capsule form, on sugar cubes, cookies, or even paper. Only occasionally is the chemical injected directly into the bloodstream.

The effects are phenomenal. The substance changes certain chemicals in the brain, with the possible result of hallucinations, intensification and distortion of sensory perception, panic, violence, insanity, and suicide. Hallucinations may recur up to two years after the original trip.

The slang terms for LSD are "acid," "sugar," "25," "the big D," "the cube," and "Lucy in the Sky and Diamonds."

Morning Glory Seeds (Rivea corymbosa)

These seeds, containing lysergic acid amide, an alkaloid derivative, have about one-tenth the potency of LSD. Although their use by addicts is comparatively recent, there is evidence that it can be traced back hundreds of years among Mexican Indians.

The main objection to all hallucinogens, including morning glory seeds, is that medical science does not know all the possible effects, and thus the user is taking great risks.

Only certain varieties of morning glory seeds are hallucinogenic. The powerful seeds can be identified by their triangular shape, whereas those that are comparatively harmless are round.

A tea is prepared with the seeds, or the drug can be extracted to get the hallucinogenic effects. The seeds can also be chewed. The results, however, are not always salutary. Vomiting, dizziness, and diarrhea are frequent reactions to the use of morning glory seeds.

Slang terms are "seeds," "glory seeds," and "Pearly Gates."

STP (4-methyl-2, 5-dimethoxy amphetamine)

STP is related to mescaline and amphetamine. It produces hallucinogenic effects that may continue for 8 to 10 hours if the dose is greater than 3 mg. The euphoria is less with a smaller dose.

There are many instances of bad trips and hospitalization from the drug, which may cause blurred vision, difficulty in swallowing, and even respiratory paralysis.

At present, the drug comes in tablet or capsule form, pink, cone-shaped. Originally, the tablets were white, blue, or peach-colored. The FDA has reported that STP is identical to "DOM," a research hallucinogenic substance. The drug is taken by mouth. Little is known of its effects from a medical point of view.

The street names for STP are "serenity," "tranquility," and "peace."

Mescaline (3,4,5-trimethoxphenylethylamine)

Mescaline is derived from the peyote cactus. The peyote is a sort of button that grows on the cactus. The drug has a long history of use by Indians in religious rituals. At present, there is little medical use of the drug.

The dry bud or button is ground into a dark brown powder, which is packed in gelatin capsules.

The effects of mescaline are like those of LSD, but more intense, particularly in visual sensations. They can last up to 12 hours. Although a few cases of intravenous injection have been reported, mescaline is nearly always taken orally. Because of its bitter taste, it is usually mixed with tea, coffee, or soda.

Street names are "peyote," "buttons," and "plants."

DMT (dimethyltryptamine)

This is a synthetic compound of triptamine. It is also a natural ingredient of various West Indian and South American plants.

The effects of DMT are similar to those of LSD but of shorter duration. A trip lasts from one to three hours.

DMT appears as a liquid or as crystals. Its color varies from bright to dirty orange, depending on its purity. In solution it is injected into a vein or into muscle. It is also soaked with marijuana and smoked.

Street names for DMT are the "businessman special" and the "lunch-hour trip."

DET (diethyltryptamine)

Similar in effects to the related DMT, DET causes reactions that last two to three hours. The drug is generally smoked mixed with tobacco, tea, parsley, or marijuana. It causes time and vision distortions.

Psilocybin (Psilocybe mexicana)

Extracted from Mexican mushrooms, psilocybin has been used by primitive societies seeking supernatural powers and communications. The effects are like those of mescaline and LSD. A dose of 20 to 60 mg. produces a trip lasting up to six hours.

Bufotenine (5-hydroxy-N, N-dimethyltryptamine)

Bufotenine is obtained from the seeds and pods of *Piptadenia peregrina*, a shrub that grows in northern South America and the West Indies. It is related to DMT. Used as a snuff, it produces intoxication and hallucinations. Indians used it to become fearless and insensitive to pain. The drug has no effect if used orally.

Ibogaine

The roots, stems, and leaves of the African shrub *Taber-nanthe iboga* provide the ingredients for ibogaine. African hunters use its extract to enable them to remain motionless for up to two days while still retaining mental alertness. The drug is used to combat fatigue; however, if taken in large doses, it causes excitement, drunkenness, mental confusion, and sometimes hallucinations.

Smash

Smash is a powerful new concoction now being sold by narcotics dealers. Marijuana is cooked with acetone to produce oil of cannabis. This oil is mixed with hashish, forming a tarlike substance, which is rolled into pellets and smoked. It is said to be manufactured in Mexico.

LBJ (JB-336-N-methyl-3 benzilate hydrochloride)

Underground newspapers have reported a new and dangerous hallucinogen, called LBJ. The effects are said to be similar to those of LSD, including hallucinations, muscle relaxation, drunkenness, and a psychotic state. Free samples are reported to have been distributed in the New York and Boston areas. The samples were in capsule and in powder form, off-white with specks of blue.

THC (delta 1, tetrahydrocannalinot)

This substance, a synthetic marijuana, is being used in medical research, making it possible to study the reactions of marijuana more objectively. The experimental drug is a colorless, odorless liquid, capable of being synthesized in any desired strength. Two or three drops on tobacco can lead to a trip lasting four to six hours.

Now you have an education in the vast field of narcotics. And you are also aware that taking that route to exorcise anxiety and loneliness has many dark by-ways that may lead to torments more tragic than the loneliness itself.

/

Part 2
THE SOLUTION

I realize that nothing in the world
is more distasteful to a man than to
take the path that leads to himself.

Demian—Herman Hesse

CHAPTER VII

What Is the Proxy Method?

You have, up to this point, observed what havoc loneliness can wreak and how many people struggle in vain to regain stability and peace of mind from their psychological dilemma. Some strike out blindly, often consulting advisers of doubtful qualifications and understanding. Others plunge into the morass of perpetual anger, drugs, and synthetic highs. The alienation and the loneliness form a dark panorama, with many lost and helpless people.

In Part 2 you are presented with a method of overcoming loneliness, which, as illustrated in the preceding chapters, has worked for many years in the privacy of a psychologist's office. It is called the Proxy Method because it involves others who actually perform the tasks that you ordinarily cannot do for yourself.

It is difficult for a person to reach a given goal toward better mental health through his own willpower. There resides in each of us a tendency to self-destruction, a force that impels us to submit to the death instinct as opposed by our drive to live—the life instinct. We want to succeed, but something within us often presses us to an opposite direction.

The person working with a psychologist in the process of therapy has a helpmate against this negative drive. Working alone for self-improvement, however, the person needs specific directions to assure that the best part of himself wins out.

A definite clue was obtained in a laboratory experiment in which a patient was asked to portray various emotions as if he were an actor playing a part. When requested to portray anger, he did so rather poorly. But when asked to instruct another patient to show signs of anger, illustrating the emotion by his own actions, he proved very effective in actually portraying that emotion. This phenomenon substantiates a well-known fact: that one learns best by teaching a subject to someone else.

The Proxy Method seeks to defeat the ambivalence created by one's negative tendencies as opposed to his positive potentialities.

What are the essentials of the Proxy Method to eliminate loneliness and other allied emotional difficulties?

1. Paradoxically, you are to forget your own loneliness or any other psychological problems you may have.
2. Instead, you will identify the psychological needs of a particular person or persons according to the instructions provided.
3. You will acknowledge that the denial or frustration of those needs is the direct cause of loneliness.
4. The next step will be through your own efforts to help to satisfy those needs in others.
5. Without directly seeking to satisfy your own needs, you will discover that your loneliness or other psychological problems have disappeared in the process.

If this formula seems complicated, it will be developed gradually and easily in the chapters to follow. And, as previously mentioned, the reward will be not only that you will be free of loneliness, but that your personality will be radically changed for the better as you blossom into a happier person.

But let us hesitate a moment; perhaps you're not too serious about achieving a happier existence without the brooding loneliness that is the lot of so many people.

We have already seen that all humans are subject not only to creativity, but also to a subconscious wish for self-destruction. As you bacome familiar with the Proxy Method, however, it will be evident that you can circumvent this tendency to harmful behavior and thus proceed without hindrance to self-improvement.

CHAPTER VIII

The Human Touch

So you're going to begin your campaign by thinking not of yourself, but of someone else. The first psychological need that you will now identify is a sense of belonging—which you will develop in someone else, not yourself.

What is a sense of belonging?

It is being touched emotionally by another person. Those people whose need for belonging is met have a feeling of being appreciated and are recognized as friendly. Accordingly, they feel worthwhile, self-respecting. Those who do not possess that important sense of belonging lack the healthy perception of being important to someone or to others. They have been denied what is important to practically all human beings, and they tend to be unhappy and lonely.

Another factor tending to loneliness in many people is the high mobility of our population. We are a nation of gypsies, with about 42 million Americans moving their place of residence at least once each year. We move about more than any other people in the world. This mobility may be one of the reasons for the increasing number of people who are indifferent to close associations because in new surroundings they find it difficult to establish relationships or learn to trust others.

Your job, under the Proxy Method, is to fulfill this need for belonging in one or more persons. You'll find it not hard as you follow the directions given in this chapter.

You must seek a lonely person who is denied the need to belong, to be accepted by neighbors, and who in consequence is not as happy as he might be.

If you happen to be in a rural area, in a small town, you will have noted a reverse migration from city life to the country.

People are dislodged from the large cities by the prevalence of crime, the loss of jobs, and the rapid technological and social changes. You will recognize the problem of those who have been uprooted from familiar environments. Understanding the difficulties of those who must adjust to a new life, you then make yourself an instrument for the elimination of their loneliness in the new surroundings.

Whereas the footlooseness of pioneers was seen as evidence of vitality in former generations, today the acceleration of mobility has become a cause of concern. As a result, many people feel unconnected to either place or people. There tends to be a breakdown of community living and an increase in social fragmentation.

One woman reports that her family has been compelled to move nine times in the last five years. Now, because of a new job for her husband, they must move once more. That means the children will have to change schools and adapt themselves to new friends again. And the future still promises other moves as the father continues to receive promotions and career advancements.

In earlier chapters, we have emphasized the psychological basis of loneliness as the accompaniment of frustrations. But purely environmental factors can be the sources of frustrations. In any case, regardless of the causes of anxiety and loneliness, the cure is the same: the satisfaction of psychological needs that can arise from actual physical hardships as well as psychological conflicts.

Your job is not to act as a psychologist or psychiatrist. According to the Proxy Method, the source of the frustration is not as important as the actual satisfaction of needs. Your present concern is merely to imbue others with a sense of belonging.

The basic assumption of the Proxy Method is borrowed from the behavioristic school of psychology so ably advocated by such national and international figures as B. F. Skinner of Harvard University.

The behavioristic principle is simple: that which is rewarded tends to be desired and sought after, while that which is punished tends to be avoided and rejected. In short, if you want to develop a given habit, attach it to something pleasant and rewarding. On the other hand, if you want to get rid of a bad habit, link it to something unpleasant and punitive.

You'll find that loneliness among your acquaintances is often associated with disability in body and spirit. Doctors every day see patients suffering from migraine headaches, skin rashes, obesity, alcoholism, and insomnia—who actually are suffering from loneliness.

As you proceed in your mission of lessening loneliness in others, you must keep in mind that positive remarks, praise, constructive suggestions, encouragement, and friendship all add up to meeting the person's need to belong. You must understand that a lonely person is often afraid to risk trusting and loving. You must take that risk yourself so that your own inhibition can be released into outgoing spontaneity.

What more specifically should you do under the Proxy Method to ameliorate loneliness?

Determine to give communication top priority. In your own family, for example, get family members to agree to talk to one another. How communicative are you with your mate? It is so easy to "turn a deaf ear" when the other person is talking about something in which you have little interest. The most common complaint of wives is that her husband does not listen, that he is concerned with his own affairs and fails to realize that by talking she is trying to establish communica-tion, closeness, in an attempt to soften her own loneliness.

In your campaign you should show your feelings, encouraging others to express their hurt, fear, sadness, and joy. These emerge from the delicate parts of an individual, and their expression strengthens a sense of belonging.

When someone blurts out his marital or job difficulties, it is easy to brush off his words with disinterest and mechanical responses such as, "But you're exaggerating—it's not so bad."

But you, as a practitioner of the Proxy Method, will understand what the complaints are about. Dodging a logical and possibly true explanation, you will simply offer sympathy, making the person feel that he is not alone, not really rejected.

By letting him tell you his troubles, you make it possible for him to be helped, reducing his disappointments. Avoid turning away the complaints with the ready remark, "You think *you* got problems." This sort of comment merely increases his problem because he then feels compelled to defend his feelings. Never belittle the other person's difficulties. As far as you are concerned, it is his feeling of frustration that is at the core of his discomfort. Increasing his sense of self-worth, his sense of belonging, his assurance of your friendship by your sympathetic listening—all are part of your design to make him feel that he is not alone.

At times, even with the best of intentions, you may find yourself arguing with members of your own family. But, if you must, argue creatively rather than in a destructive manner. This involves dealing only with issues, never with personalities. Speak for yourself, and do not presume to think for the other person. Never say, "You make me angry," or "You hurt me." Such remarks are construed as unfair because they overlook the issue.

You'll discover that many people tend to hide their emotions. When angry, for example, they repress that feeling lest they become violent and hurt someone. Others repress their love out of fear of being rejected, abandoned. Those who repress their emotions consistently are judged to be "cold fish," making it difficult for them to develop friendships and intimate relationships.

By understanding the dynamics operating in repressed persons, you will be guided in the technique of conveying a sense of belonging.

Ask others how they feel about things. In that way, you'll initiate conversations touching upon feelings, thus stimulating responses.

Confide in others, thus encouraging them to confide in you. Many people hesitate to hear the problems of others because they do not want to become involved. You can advantageously encourage friends to confide in you and ventilate their feelings without appearing to be nosy or gossipy. Be tactful and constructive in your discussions, thus deepening trust and friendship.

Visit people when they're troubled. Sometimes, often

erroneously, it is assumed that people want to be left alone when ill, bereaved, or in traumatic situations. Accordingly, you can be of real help to the majority of these people.

Be free with compliments. There are good qualities in everybody. You need not flatter or deceive in order to enhance a spirit of belonging. You stress the socially desirable qualities instead of the weaknesses. However, it is well to be selective in paying compliments. To be strictly honest may be a form of dishonesty, a destructive form of communication. Avoid the rationalization of the person who holds that he must always tell the truth no matter how it may hurt someone else; he may be acting on his own weaknesses and neurosis in his communications. For example, a person may confess adultery, feeling that he must be honest, while actually he is indulging a subconscious desire to hurt his mate.

A husband, however, who compliments his wife when he likes what she's wearing encourages her to wear what he likes, says Dr. Herbert M. Herbert, former professor of psychology at Pepperdine University in Los Angeles. The likely result, he proposes, is that the wife will return the compliment not only by wearing more often what her husband likes but also by being more affectionate.

Pay compliments only when they are deserved. Be specific. Instead of saying, "You look nice today," you can say, "Your blouse is becoming; it matches your eyes." Be tactful; don't come on too strong with people you do not know well.

Dr. Ira J. Tanner, psychologist, says, "A lonely person is afraid to risk loving people." You must take this risk and help others take it to overcome loneliness.

Friendship is the cement that binds people to one another. It shuts out alienation and loneliness, yielding a sense of the universally sought after belonging.

Studies show that a person's ability to make lasting friendships tends to go with a general capacity to evaluate people correctly. You should be aware, in order to help others, that making friends is simple. Friendships grow out of acquaintance. That is the secret. You encourage the lonely person to increase casual contacts. Out of these will come friendships, and sooner or later the person will find a real relationship.

A good friendship is one in which each person has sized up the other, realizing finally that there is more to like than to dislike. Each also wants happiness and growth for the other. Each wants to communicate his thoughts, feelings, memories, and beliefs. And further each wants to be understood by the other and strives for that understanding.

There is a difference between friendship and love. The difference lies in degree of intensity. One feels comfortable with a friend, whereas the emotion of love reaches a deeper and more fixed attachment. One should not assume that all friendship must inevitably lead to love, although many friendships do develop into the deeper emotional state.

Of course, you will encounter people who are incapable of a sincere and honest relationship, perhaps because of a psychological problem, but also because they insist on presenting a phony facade, projecting a false self that they believe will be acceptable to others. By not being themselves, they actually set up barriers that prevent the meeting of minds and spirits. We need friends, nevertheless, to avoid loneliness, to feel that precious sense of belonging. Only then can we attain satisfying lives.

In your mission to imbue friendship in others, it is well for you to realize that the best-liked people are those who like others. People who express mainly negative attitudes tend to be disliked, whereas those who express mainly positive opinions tend to be liked.

One young woman had been filled with dreams of living a glamorous life as a career girl in New York City. But having taken the plunge into the new surroundings, months later she felt very much alone and had drifted into discouragement. The thought of suicide slipped into her mind. She couldn't stand the loneliness anymore. "I'll end this rotten life," she told herself. For a long time, she gazed from her apartment window upon the throng below. Music drifted upward from a nearby hotel. Gradually the death wish began to vanish. Suddenly it dawned on her that it wasn't New York that had rejected her. She realized that her problem was that she had made no efforts to make friends. In her shyness and unduly high expectations, she had repelled others with an aura of coldness.

She gave herself a pep talk. No longer would she remain glued to the television set; she would actively seek out people, acquaintances. She had to learn how to care for others, to be honest and open with them.

She joined an organization, became involved in its activities, signed up as a volunteer for a charity, and ultimately enrolled in an adult education class. Her determination paid off in several friendships, and life became full of excitement and companionship. She felt a strong sense of belonging and made friends wherever she went because of her new attitudes.

However, not every lonely person can arrange life as successfully. It is here that you can provide leadership by yourself being a true friend. From then on, you'll see the person gradually enlarging his or her circle, sparked by your sincere and sympathetic encouragement.

But what about the person who rejects your offer of friendship? The fact is that you can turn even hostile neighbors into friends. You can do this by being the first to make overtures, such as doing small favors, inviting the person to your home. Of course, you must not overdo flattery. If you seem overanxious, your motives may be suspected.

Respect other people's privacy. Rather find out their interests. For example, get a person to talk about himself. If he is interested in art or painting, ask him which are the best museums, what he thinks of certain artists. People tend to like those who are sympathetic listeners. By all means resist the temptation to boast about yourself; bragging puts people off. And certainly keep your problems to yourself and out of the conversation. Remind yourself that others have different values and opinions. You need not argue with everything said, but instead show interest in the other's point of view.

Remember that shyness is widely prevalent among those with whom you come in contact. Avoid particularly the idea that other people are constantly examining you and making judgments, and don't worry about the possibility that you will not be liked. In fact, in proceeding with your aim for friendship, you become more human, more likeable, and therefore more effective in meeting the need to belong.

When you have devoted about a week to satisfying and meeting the needs of others, an unexpected transformation begins to take place in your own life. You are a different person; somehow, as you have led others toward accepting your guidance, positive attitudes, and encouragement, you find yourself closer to people, more accepted and appreciated.

You are no longer alone.

The Proxy Method has begun to work. You are gradually being more popular and sought after because no longer are you self-centered. You make people feel happier. And the miracle is that in the process you have accomplished what so many others attempt in vain. By being unselfish, forgetting about yourself in the service of others, you have realized the most selfish aim of all—a sense of belonging, a feeling of self-worth and self-respect, and the elimination of loneliness.

The principle of "casting your bread upon the waters" with the assurance that it will be returned to you a thousandfold is basic in all major religions. More ruthless people, particularly in the advertising business, know that appearing to offer something for nothing entices buyers to the marketplace.

A character trait in many of us impels us toward the magic of receiving without giving. This mind-set is the basis of all gambling, the motive of all lottery ticket buyers.

Of course, in seeking to meet the needs of others for belonging and sharing, you are not utilizing the cupidity of others. You are harnessing the best in humankind by offering a helping hand—knowing that kindness tends to be reciprocated.

CHAPTER IX

Self-Worth

Of the millions of workers in this country, most are unhappy at their jobs, says author Studs Terkei. They suffer from headaches, backaches, ulcers, alcoholism, drug addiction, and nervous breakdowns. They are unsatisfied, Terkel continues, because they consider their jobs a form of violence. It robs them of their self-worth and of a feeling of accomplishment.

In other words, millions have little to give them a sense of achievement, a psychological need that is universal in human beings.

What these people desire is meaningful work that will bring them recognition and pride. They crave activities that will enhance their inner life, give them a sense that their existence is not in vain, that the world knows that they live and breathe. They want to reach out beyond themselves, to gain a sense of achievement that identifies them as contributors to their environment to escape the loneliness that always threatens their lives. That loneliness lurks ever ready to pounce upon them, on all who are alienated and frustrated.

The executive commuting day after day rises at 5 a.m., nursing a hangover or an ulcer. He always thought that one promotion after another would bring the satisfaction that he sought. And yet the ulcer and the free-floating anxiety will not go away. His need for achievement remains unfulfilled.

At the same time, a farm worker feels that he cannot take it anymore. Standing at 105 degrees in the shade, he views seemingly endless rows of lettuce. And his back hurts. His sense of achievement is practically nil, and within him is a gnawing loneliness.

An assembly-line worker stands on the spot, moving no more than two or three feet during the whole day. The only time he can stop is when the assembly line stops. The man's sense of achievement is something that is beyond him.

The bus driver suffers from hemorrhoids and kidney trouble. Little wonder that, without a sense of achievement, he is often not as courteous as he might be.

The fashion model certainly should feel satisfaction in her work. Yet she feels often that she is nothing but a clothes rack. One customer calls her great, and another tells her that she is terrible. One moment it's acceptance, the next it is rejection.

Beyond the widespread dissatisfaction among workers is the fear of losing the job, not being needed, being replaced by someone else or by a machine.

However, the negative factors stressed by writers such as Terkel may not be the essential element in the worker's dissatisfaction. We are dealing, not with a job, but with an unmet need, the need for a sense of achievement to offset the always potential loneliness. A man or woman who has a happy home life, with love and a sense of belonging, often finds the most tedious job highly satisfactory.

You already have encouraged a feeling of belonging during the first week of your campaign, which by producing a sense of worth will make it easier to go on to your second task, the imbuing of a sense of achievement. This psychological need can be satisfied not only on the job, but also at school, in social activities, and with hobbies. We are dealing with a psychological factor rather than with a given occupation.

It has been demonstrated, for example, that 70 percent of the loss of jobs is not attributable to lack of skill or efficiency, but rather to personality deficiencies. The person whom you wish to influence positively, if he happens not to be employed, can be shown that the need for achievement is reachable in many activities. Although you may stress employment, the principles of job satisfaction are the same for application in other areas.

As far as jobs are concerned, it is well to point out to the person the pitfalls that prevent the feeling of achievment in the workplace. Vocational guidance specialists agree with the suggestions that follow.

Make sure that the boss is aware of your talents and skills that might be beneficial to the firm. In demonstrating photography, for example, arrange your display with great care particularly slanted to the interests and potential profitability of the company involved.

Don't waste time on people who are without direction or rationale toward worthwhile goals. You can use that time more advantageously to learn, to produce more on the job.

Remember to express appreciation when a superior or co-worker offers compliments or praise for a task well done.

Give the appearance of being enthusiastic about your work even when you have an inclination to resent a given task. Look for something different about the assignment to lend it new meaning.

Punctuality is very important when people are sizing up your personality. Don't be a clock watcher. Be prompt in reporting for work or attending meetings.

Don't be too much of a yes-man, but when you disagree, explain your opinion firmly but pleasantly. To agree with everybody marks you as lacking in discrimination or strength of character. Learn as much as possible about the firm and the jobs of co-workers. This provides a solid foundation for career advancement.

Be a good listener. Pay close attention when given instruction or directions. To listen is as important as to speak up when the occasion warrants. It is an indication of having self-control and avoids the fault of undue self-importance.

Learn the interests of fellow-workers, thus laying the foundation for mutual sharing and meaningful conversations, making you an agreeable person capable of leadership.

These recommendations of guidance counselors to industry should be passed on by you to those who would seek to develop a feeling of achievement. They will make a person stand out in his job and thereby meet that psychological need that everyone feels.

Even under the best of circumstances, however, many factors may hinder a person from carrying out some of these recommendations. If you are to talk intelligently in your efforts to encourage a sense of achievement in another person, you should be familiar with the state of mind of many workers that tends to dull ideas of achievement on the job. "Do you like your job?" How many answered in the negative?

A recent survey revealed that workers want more. More what? More money? No. They want more satisfaction out of their jobs, more of a sense of achievement. Lacking this psychological need, many employees respond with negative and destructive behavior, including absenteeism, alcoholism, low morale, high turnover, careless workmanship, theft, and sometimes even sabotage.

The survey also showed that 44 percent of all workers questioned reported that they felt trapped in their jobs.

The magazine *Psychology Today* conducted an extensive survey of working men and women, disclosing the need for a sense of achievement expressed as follows:

They want more opportunities to develop their talents and skills, a chance to participate in decision-making affecting policies and conditions of their work; they want to accomplish something worthwhile.

Industrial psychologists assert that the malaise of today's workers is largely because they are more self-oriented. One sociologist observed that people are more interested in having a satisfying job than they are in social reforms.

More and more workers are expressing what makes them unhappy, indicating a widespread unmet need for a sense of achievement. Among their specific resentments are being made to feel like robots, being watched and spied upon, being treated like idiot children, and having no control over their working lives.

One steel worker, quoted in Studs Terkel's book *Working*, expressed the melancholy, the loneliness, that runs beneath the surface of the working world. "Everybody should have something he can point to," he said. "Picasso can point to a painting. A writer can point to a book. What can I point to?"

How well that steel worker expressed the universal need for a sense of achievement to save him from the loneliness of unfulfillment.

Before you will be in a position to guide another person

toward overcoming his difficulties on the job, it is necessary that you know some of the fallacies about the workplace and many employees.

For example, a popular myth is that manual and low-status laborers as a group are the least happy in society. In fact, professionals and technical employees are the least satisfied.

It is also assumed that workers want more pay above all else. Again, that is untrue. The National Commission on Manpower Policy has found that, given the opportunity to choose, they prefer more leisure time.

Still another fallacy, according to the survey, is that workers are always bored and unhappy at factory jobs or on the assembly line. The truth is that the monotony of these jobs provides the chance to gossip and daydream, activities valued by some workers.

It is interesting to discover that winning a million-dollar lottery or otherwise suddenly becoming rich does not automatically lead the worker from his job. The fact is that three out of four insist on continuing to work even though there is no longer a financial incentive.

Most people, it is assumed, would jump at the opportunity to accept a high-paying position even though the work does not interest them. But in actuality two out of three would refuse to make the trade.

The facts thus far presented in this chapter seem contradictory. The thread, however, that runs through the differing opinions and attitudes is of the same color, indicating the lack of a sense of achievement as the chief cause of disillusionment, boredom, and a pervading loneliness.

The job scene is certainly important as an area where the need for achievement may be met. But equally important are the many other opportunities to achieve outside the job—in the home, among friends, in hobbies, church, clubs, and numerous other outlets.

When the economy makes the job market precarious, it is important that you become aware of these substitutes available outside the place of employment in your campaign to engender a sense of achievement.

One of the principles to keep in mind is that a person tends to be happy when he does something he finds enjoyable. People who are vitally absorbed in an activity find themselves more adequate. It is therefore your task in influencing another person to discover what he is interested in and if possible to join him in that activity. Discovering other potentially satisfying activities will broaden his horizon.

If you suggest some sport or activity and find that your client—let's call him your client—comes up with an elaborate rationalization for not doing what you suggest, it may be that he is afraid of failure, afraid of being awkward, foolish, of making mistakes.

One young man, for example, was fascinated by the mechanical aspects of cars. But feeling inadequate with things mechanical, he had never done anything about that interest. When it was suggested that he try, he responded that he would never be any good with cars. His advisor brought some auto parts, which they discussed in his backyard, comparing them with the parts in his own car. Then he was given material to read about cars. Ultimately he lost his fear of failing as a mechanic and became immersed in cars. Finally, he planned to become an automobile mechanic as a career. He had admitted to himself that he wasn't as gauche as he had assumed. Doing something he had thought beyond his capability boosted his self-image and led to a sense of achievement, which also spread to other areas of his life.

Recommend to your client that he itemize a list of things he enjoys doing. That will make him more aware of his whole range of interests and tempt him to experiment with some of them. Try to persuade him to tackle something new. If you participate with him in such a venture, he will feel less hesitant, less afraid of failure. Urge him not to make excuses. Getting started is the main part of the battle.

Similarly, arrange to have him meet new people. A person who hesitates to go out on his own is encouraged when accompanied by a friend. As he meets new people, he expands his horizon and interests.

Encourage your client to read newspapers to widen his view of the world and make him feel that he is part of many things outside himself.

Possibly your client could do volunteer work with some organization, church, school, hospital, nursing home, charity drive. Volunteering can do much to create a sense of contribution and achievement.

An increasingly popular way to meet people is taking adult education courses, returning to college classes at night or on weekends or taking added training in a junior college or a business school. The engendering of a sense of growth both vocationally and intellectually provides a lift to one's ego.

Do not push your client too hard. Lead him gradually. Small success leads to greater successes through augmenting self-confidence.

If you dislike yourself, you have set up a negativism that is projected to other people, who in return may dislike you, paying you back in your own destructive currency. On the other hand, if you feel good about yourself you have most likely met your psychological need for a sense of achievement, concomitantly gaining self-confidence.

If your client is inclined to belittle himself, he should be urged to stop fault-finding. He must never say, "I'm too dumb to do that," or "I couldn't do that." Of course, this admonition must recognize individual differences and limitations. To have a person with an I.Q. of 76 aspire to become an astronaut is a false evaluation of reality.

Nevertheless, when evaluating one's talents, it's surprising how much better a person feels when he stops running himself down. With this change, the person can follow up with reasonable and positive action.

If you are dissatisfied with your personal appearance, you can determine to do something about it. This can involve new clothes, change in hair style, and a general sprucing up of personal habits. You can be taught not to slouch, sitting with limbs awry, but to stand straight, resulting in greater self-pride. Just trying to help oneself will result in improved self-esteem.

No one is without some talents. The individual must recognize his own abilities. When a person makes a dress, paints a picture, devises a new recipe, or bakes a cake, that person is being creative. But you shouldn't compare your achievements with those of an expert in the field. Measure yourself by your own standards.

You must guard against an unconscious tendency to set goals so high as to assure failure. An example might be the journalist who, being very successful as a newspaper man or woman, yet aspires to write the great American novel. He may be highly competent in evaluating details, meticulous in organizing material, yet devoid of ability to inject the emotional content required in a novel. He has set his goal too high because of failure to assess his talents correctly—thus almost assuring inadequate performance.

Once a success is achieved, however, the person should keep reminding himself of that success. Put aside past failures. You will soon be able to see in your client differences in his appearance, in personality. He has acquired a sense of achievement, changing him into a new person endowed with dynamics that augur improvement in his existence.

The suggestions made in this chapter are not sacrosanct. In fact, you may substitute your own or other procedures that may prove highly effective. The application of one or two items may be sufficient to accomplish your purpose. After all, you have only so much time to devote to this task. The important thing is to maintain an awareness of your goal. With such an attitude, you'll find the application of the Proxy Method almost automatic. The main point to remember is that your goal is to engender a sense of achievement in someone else. At times, this may involve merely uttering a few words of praise and encouragement.

So far, we have made some progress in the application of the Proxy Method. Succinctly restated, it is the use of others to reach your own goal. You have been warned to put aside your own needs and problems. For the time being, you are merely concerned to help others—in this case, to gain satisfaction of the need to achieve.

But as you have turned your thoughts and actions to the welfare of others, a strange thing has happened. Without thinking of yourself, your own need for achievement has been fulfilled. In fact, you could not have followed the directions of the Proxy Method without reaping considerable benefit.

How contrary this approach is to the self-willed decision to meet your own needs. You may otherwise promise to perform certain acts and refrain from others, but almost inevitably the perverse demon in you—the death instinct—defeats you. With the Proxy Method, in a circuitous manner you avoid the negative and destructive impulse. It's as if you thus defeat the perversity within your subconscious by saying, "Why try to pull me down when I'm not working for myself but for others, and therefore do not deserve punishment." Before your subconscious becomes aware of the trick you have played on it, your own triumph has already occurred. And furthermore, by satisfying the need for achievement in others, you have accomplished almost surreptitiously a creative and worthwhile act—a process that has automatically brought you a deep sense of achievement.

Tricking the subconscious is fascinating. Deep within you are a variety of impulses that may dominate your behavior without your awareness. These impulses are remnants of your childhood, defenses that are not appropriate to adult life. For example, temper tantrums may have achieved what you wanted when you were little, but such behavior is no longer effective in influencing other people.

In seeking to convey a sense of achievement in another person, you must recognize that subconcious factors often determine likes and dislikes. Your task is not to analyze these tendencies, but rather to encourage further development in those areas that are of interest in the here and now. Not all subconscious motives are bad. You must allow your client to do what gives him a sense of achievement as long as it doesn't harm others.

CHAPTER X

Lessening Fears

Research has shown that fear can be destructive to the body. It can produce a chemical change in the blood.

Basically the emotion of being afraid is a psychological device to warn the organism that it is threatened by something dangerous, real or imagined. When thus confronted, the person becomes tense and, obeying innate mechanisms, prepares for a struggle, to fight for survival. In our society, the primitive tendency to become violent against threatening possibilities is generally suppressed, but the chemical action within the body remains. The physiological being is ready to fight, the glands secrete their juices, the muscles tighten. The feeling is that of an animal caught in a trap or a person strapped in a straitjacket. The resultant frustration is tremendous, creating anxiety, anger, and guilt that contribute to the alienation felt as loneliness.

Shyness is a form of fear, the fear of rejection, or more subtly of one's conscience. Many research projects have shown the great prevalence of that emotion. A recent study reveals that 14 percent of elementary children are shy; in junior high school the proportion rises to 24 percent, and in senior high it drops to 12 percent. Although the reported number of shy students in universities is set at 5 percent, many sociologists say that the current percentage is much higher.

The fear known as shyness is defined by Gerald Phillips, an expert on overcoming shyness. "What we mean by shy," he says "is that they are sufficiently guilty and withdrawn to suffer penalties." Shy people are afraid to recite in class or speak before other groups; they even recoil from conversations with strangers, not to mention being tongue-tied with friends. Contrary to a notion that bashful people are often dumb, the fact is that many have been found more talented than average.

The fear of communication is a definite hindrance to progress on the job. You can, for example, have great technical skills, but if you're not able to communicate with superiors and fellow-workers, you are frequently passed over for promotions, creating added frustration.

Obviously there is a field for the cultivation of your efforts to help others lessen their shyness.

The fear experienced by some Vietnam veterans is often manifested in the form of terrible nightmares. It is understandable that the war experiences are so painful that the veterans prefer not to talk about the past. Yet, if one of your clients is in that category, it is necessary to get him to speak, to say aloud the details of the terror that still swirls in his mind.

You can stress that no one can simply forget his fears. They must be brought into the open. The shattering emotion must be ventilated; otherwise, it remains and only comes to the surface in the form of nightmares. It is not unusual for this psychological problem to emerge even years after the actual experiences. There is often a residue of guilt because one is a survivor while his buddies died.

You can help in this situation by quiet understanding, by minimizing pressures, and by constant reassurance of love and respect.

Of course, the recommendations are equally valid with anyone suffering from traumatic experiences in civilian life. This, for example, would include those suffering from phobias, the torments of which may be severe.

Phobic fear breeds numerous difficulties for the victim, and at times it seems almost equally irksome to family members and acquaintances. People suffer from phobias in various degree of severity. The average person may be moderately afraid of dogs and cross the street to avoid the animal. But another person afflicted with a crippling fear of dogs will break out in a cold sweat, gripped by terror.

There are many types of phobias. The most common are fear of heights, fear of enclosed space, and fear of open places.

The victim of claustrophobia (fear of enclosed space) will avoid elevators and will shy away from crowds for fear of being unable to break free from the throng of people.

The person who is subject to agoraphobia (fear of open places) suffers spontaneous attacks of panic with heart palpitation, dry mouth, and an overwhelming feeling that he is about to die on the spot. The victim therefore wants to be reassured that someone will be there to help and accordingly becomes very demanding, refusing to travel alone. The open spaces symbolize being abandoned.

Some women with agoraphobia become housebound, their fear merging with a tenacious loneliness. Schoolchildren refuse to attend classes, dreading to leave home. Family members and friends rarely understand the tyrannical demands of the sufferer.

Phobic fears frequently develop following disturbances, changes, bereavement, hysterectomy. It has been theorized that a phobia is a cry for help, a signal of the need to be mothered, a demand for the unquestioned love sought by a helpless child. People with phobias are said to have rich inner resources, great imagination and creativity. They are also people whose abilities are underutilized and isolated.

You, as the exponent of the Proxy Method to lessen or eliminate phobic fears, can do as much as the typical psychotherapist if you apply a few simple rules.

Have the victim understand his symptoms. Assuming that a doctor has found no organic problems, you can assure the person that there is nothing wrong with his heart or head or other part of his body, that he can confront his fears knowing that he is not having a heart attack or a fainting spell.

Urge your client to accept his feelings, to bear with them. His is not going crazy, nor is there a possibility that he will do so. Finally point out that there are a million others who suffer from the same phobia. He should not seek to control his feelings, because that merely aggravates them. He should remember that he is responding to a threat that is unreal. Instead, he should fix his attention on his immediate environment, noticing particular objects and concentrating on them.

Recommend that your client learn to relax. Taking deep

breaths, he can think of the breathing itself, not of the fear. Let him imagine a scene of serenity in which he can see himself whenever the panic threatens.

Then comes the desensitization of the feared object or situation. This means that the victim gradually approaches what he fears, at first only in his imagination. Let him visualize the object of his fear, gradually becoming more accustomed to it. If he is afraid of dogs, for example, let him think of the animal, then possibly look at a picture of one, ultimately working toward looking at the real thing in the street and finally touching one. The fear becomes desensitized when the person can confront his fear, knowing that he is not having a heart attack or a fainting spell. The same technique can be utilized for any phobia to eliminate the object's power to engender fear.

A phobia is obstinate in its influence over its victim. There will be setbacks, but the practice of desensitizing is being used effectively all over the country to restore numbers of people to a happier existence.

Fears are countless and occur in a variety of forms or situations. Possibly the most bizarre is the fear of success. For the average person, this fear seems incongruous. How can a person actually be afraid of good fortune, promotions, financial success, and a host of situations so commonly considered desirable?

This enigma is wrapped in psychological dynamics and conflicts little known to the normal person. "Poor Harry," a neighbor may commiserate, "whatever the man undertakes is bound to turn out all wrong—perhaps Harry was born unlucky."

What sane person would shun success?

Wouldn't it be surprising if most of us somehow became victims of that strange symptom? Our ambivalence is revealed when we undermine our best efforts, doing dumb things like arriving late for work, forgetting an appointment, a social engagement. These may be means of managing to keep success away.

We may counter that it is ridiculous to assume that we fear success. Upon closer examination, however, we may find some hidden force within ourselves brought out by questions such as "Are you afraid of making mistakes; do you feel that there is something fraudulent about yourself; are you a perfectionist?"

The phenomenon is far from rare. Often fear of success leads to tragedy, possibly exemplified in prominent people such as Judy Garland, John Belushi, and Richard Nixon. It seems indicated that success fearers tend to be high achievers; in any case, they are very sensitive people.

This fear is a defense against possible failure, an insurance against disappointment. Bad things are about to happen; somehow it is more acceptable to sleep through a given hour than to risk failure in an exam.

People who have a low sense of self-worth often feel guilty about success, assuming that they do not deserve it. But you need not be a Freudian analyst to help others lessen that fear. In fact, all that is necessary are two basic principles: 1) practically all emotional disorders are caused by being denied psychological needs, and 2) the disorders can therefore be eliminated in most instances by meeting those needs. Among them is the need to be free of fears.

Your task, therefore, is simple enough. You merely seek to remove fear of success in the person chosen as your client. Specifically, you will consider the following actions:

Help him to define his idea of success. Is it really his own or that of someone else, a parent, a sensational model? Or is his concept of success based upon what he really wants?

Have him question his assumptions. Are they based on rationalization, such as "I'm not attractive enough" for a given occupation. Is his reasoning actually a cop-out because he has too low an estimate of himself?

Although you are not overly concerned about the psychological dynamics involved, you might have your client examine some parts of his family relationships. Was he ridiculed for making mistakes during his growing years? Had he always felt that an older brother was the favorite, with parental emphasis on that sibling's superiority and talent? Is he too much influenced by negative factors in his childhood?

Are your client's aspirations unrealistic? Does he want to be a scientist when he repeatedly fails in science courses? Try to analyze his attitudes and help him to reorient his thoughts if they are obviously unrealistic and unwarranted.

Has he a fixed idea that happiness can be attained only in a given channel? Explain that everything is not lost if he cannot, for example, gain admission to an Ivy League school. He must learn to accept some failures because they are part of life.

Have him focus on enjoying day-to-day living rather than being entirely occupied with future goals. Certainly he should try to avoid self-hate, the great destroyer. Have him find things in which he now excels and enlarge upon them, thus reinforcing a sense of achievement.

Renatus Hartogs, associate director of the American Institute for Psychotherapy and Psychoanalysis, says that "...to beat the fears that hold you back in life is relatively simple."

First, it should be understood that everyone has fears. The problem becomes acute when a fear prevents a person from doing his job and interferes in relationships with others. It can destroy love and companionship.

According to Hartogs, one should act and do something about the fears. This, of course, is not in contradiction of some of the recommendations already made. However, again we must argue that the individual may simply freeze, and that his illness is specifically that he resignedly accepts his state of helplessness.

Here we come to a more realistic course of action under the Proxy Method. We do not merely offer platitudes, but rather provide direct help to have the victim meet his need for support with specific directions instead of vague and generalized advice "...to do something."

It is true that many people feel trapped in their fears. They do not have the courage to act by themselves. Many are impelled to sit at home, imbibing tranquilizers or alcohol in vain to allay their discomfort. When such a person hears the platitude that the only thing he has to fear is fear itself, he agrees totally. It is no help because that is exactly what he does fear. What he is afraid of is indeed the fear of the panic inextricably bound with the fear. The cop-out by the naive adviser therefore makes little impact on the sufferer. He interprets the advice the way the hypochondriac does that of the physician who tells him that there is nothing wrong with him. "It's all in your head," is the cruel diagnosis. Of course, the person knows that the trouble is in his head. But the fact is that his illness is indeed "in his head" and, contrary to the flip remark of the doctor, it can kill him. The pain is real. The doctor might have been more honest if he had admitted that the ailment was of a psychological nature, a field generally outside his competency.

Platitudes have never cured any emotional disorder. Frankness by the medical profession should warrant acknowledgment of their ignorance in such matters. At least with such honesty, the patient can hope to obtain the help he needs from another quarter.

It is not disgraceful to be afraid. But there are not enough competent psychiatrists and clinical psychologists to minister to the millions whose fears are a terrible burden.

Here is where the Proxy Method steps in, serving at least two persons at the same time: the helper and the person being helped.

People who suffer from severe fears yearn to share their feelings with others. They certainly do not want to hear that their miseries are all in their head or that the fears exist only in their imagination. But people learn from one another; and fears examined in the open with another person become less of a burden. Sharing diminishes them.

Again, you, as a practitioner of the Proxy Method, are discovering the old principle that one learns best by teaching others. By helping another person, you gradually understand more about yourself. While your goal was to alleviate the suffering of others, by helping them to meet their need to be free of fears you probably found that your own fears have almost magically lessened.

The many suggestions made in this chapter are at your disposal, but it must not be assumed that you must follow all of them. If you keep in mind that your primary goal is helping another person to get rid of fears, you may evolve your own devices that are as effective if not even more effective than those here presented.

The magic, of course, will be the indirect effects that your unselfishness has wrought in your own peace of mind, an erosion of your fears, and a subtle but noticeable change in your personality.

We are familiar with the widely accepted scientific finding that we are born with only two fears: the fear of falling and of loud noise. All other fears have been learned.

Most of our fears, therefore, have been imposed upon us not only as a means of avoiding danger, but also to serve the selfish interests of others. A dictatorship, for example, seeks to engender fear of weakness because it needs physically strong people to fight its wars. However, most fears creep up on us without our knowing their origins. We also tend to "inherit" our fears in the sense that we imitate the behavior of our parents.

In any case, it must be emphasized that most fears are learned, and anything learned can be unlearned. It is your task as a practitioner of the Proxy Method to help eliminate unreasonable and destructive fears.

CHAPTER XI

Lessening Guilt

According to psychologist Carl G. Jung, ideas that are part of our inheritance have clung to our subconscious to influence our lives without our being aware of them. In that category may be the universality of a sense of guilt. Everybody feels guilty at one time or other.

To link guilt to a deep current flowing from our ancestors may be interesting and valid. But it might cause us to dismiss guilt as inevitable, as something imposed on us. To struggle against it, like the original sin idea, would therefore be useless.

Modern psychologists, while not necessarily contradicting Jung, yet pragmatically would rather analyze specific and more immediate causes of guilt.

It has been observed that all emotional disturbances are due to frustration. That is the beginning and sole cause of the sense of guilt as far as we can determine by actual experience. This is not to discount entirely the possibility that the conflicts giving birth to frustration can be on the subconscious level. Regardless of the source of the frustration, our own observation and experience reveal that frustration causes anxiety. That anxiety makes us want to do something to get rid of it. But whatever we may attempt to do in that direction often fails. This failure is frequently because what we do is self-defeating. Gradually, if not suddenly, we become irritable and hostile. It has been noted, for example, that some people turn to drugs to escape anxiety. And frequently the addict becomes angry and even violent.

Inevitably, however, if the anger is repressed, it is then turned against the self. There is a diminishing of self-worth and a conviction that the person deserves punishment. At this point, the sense of guilt becomes alive and corrosive. And so the inevitable course of events follows: the anxiety merges with anger, and finally guilt.

Accordingly, we have a basis, a practical approach that works to help someone to meet his need to be free of guilt, to provide ways of removing the guilt—and the frustration disappears. Everything falls into place.

Guilt feelings are aroused by our culture through the mass media—radio, television, movies, newspapers, and magazines. The field of advertising is committed to making us feel guilty in order to sell goods. There seems to be a sort of conspiracy to make us feel unsatisfied by afflicting us with guilt because of being denied their wares.

This vast and concerted effort to make us feel guilty is to perpetuate a hang-up: the unhappy situation of making a "bad impression." If we are to be accepted by others, we must guard against body odor and countless other aspects natural to human beings. Enormous amounts are expended on ads for soap, cosmetics, bad breath remedies, and lotions to make us smell good. The devices to create guilt because we must not dare be different from others are innumerable. If we do not pay unreasonable prices for a pair of cheap jeans, we simply are not "with it." We are damned, guilty of making a poor impression.

This fear of projecting a negative impression may leave a person with self-blame. He feels that somehow it is his own fault if he is not in the groove. This attitude makes it practically impossible for him to be at ease with others.

Of course, there are measures to arrest the anger and the resentment, and having eliminated that hostility, the guilt will have vanished. A basic need will have been met—the need to be free of guilt.

Let's see how one can get at guilt, lessen it by attacking anger, which of course was its precursor. We must recall that frustration has its origin in the denial of psychological needs. Our task at this point is to attack anger, which is the twin of guilt. Get rid of anger and guilt has no longer a reason for existence.

A bad conscience is nothing but one's desire to escape from anger. But that emotion cannot be repressed for long. It must in one way or another be released, find an outlet.

So now it is your job to help a client get rid of his anger, thus indirectly getting guilt out of the way. He would thus satisfy his need to be free of his bad conscience.

You'll find that one who has not been able to handle his anger has ultimately turned that hostility against himself. He may as a consequence be suffering from headaches, back-aches, or stomach disorders or have indulged in alcohol or drug abuse. Since he cannot act out his anger, you must devise ways of diffusing it.

You may allow yourself to be used as the target of the negative feeling. Let your client attempt direct confrontation. Encourage him or even goad him into speaking his mind. If you are the one who thus invites his venom, urge him to scream and curse at you. You are the one who made him mad. Now, this will not work if you respond in kind. If you find that the procedure is obnoxious to you, it will not be effective. He can, of course, be given an explanation of your action once he has ventilated his anger.

Your client has not been punished for his irrational behav-ior, and better still, he has not been punished for his action. No longer does he feel guilty, because a sort of love and understanding have resulted, leaving him greatly relieved. This has probably never happened to him before. And inci-dentally you yourself have proven great strength of character in the process. Instead of hitting back and increasing his guilt, you provided a calm explanation.

It is possible that you may influence the angry person to turn his hostile energy to energy for self-improvement. This can be an effective device, particularly if you accompany your client in the effort. An example would be asking the person to take an evening course with you. With both of you profiting, the angry person could appreciate the gain in knowledge and skills.

Engaging in sports and other physical activities with your client can serve to redirect his hostile tendencies. Whether it be a game of tennis or using a punching bag, the energy expended becomes a catharsis for the anger.

One method utilized in the psychologist's office is to have the patient write a long letter addressed to someone whom he hates. The letter is read aloud in the presence of the therapist and destroyed after it has served its purpose. It has provided an outlet and is no longer needed.

You can, of course, help your client to confront his guilt directly. Sharing and analyzing his guilt is a constructive process. Is his guilt realistic? Has the person actually done something wrong? Are his standards too high? Or is he too much a conformist? Is he blowing up out of proportion some minor transgression? If he has done something really wrong, can he reprimand himself, consoling his conscience with determination not to repeat the offense?

Remember that sharing is in itself a psychological need. Listening sympathetically, arriving at some conclusion with someone else, conveys a sense of belonging that also helps to lessen guilt.

Dr. Wyane Dyer, author of *Your Erroneous Zones*, says that one must recognize the preposterousness of worry and guilt. Ask yourself, "Is there anything that will ever change as a result of one's worrying about it?"

Nothing can be changed by guilt to alter the past or the future. Anyway, what is deemed wrong in one generation is often acceptable and even desirable in the next. To be a slave to current fads of morality is a sort of slavery to the status quo. Conscience certainly serves a purpose of retaining the good in our society, but it can also be a tool for projecting the narrow-mindedness of neurotic people. Their rationalizations frequently are a mere means of domination to protect their own fears and guilts. Therefore, helping your client break away from the deadening norms no longer justified in our day may free him from unjustified guilts.

On the other hand, your client can be made aware of the fact that no one is perfect. Make clear that anyone who never steps out of line is long dead emotionally. Being perfect at all times is not realistic. Scolding oneself for errors is senseless.

Everybody makes mistakes. Freedom of conscience is to have the capability to determine your own rules as long as others are not hurt by the application of your scale of values.

If you have followed some of these suggestions, or substituted your own devices to enhance the satisfaction of another person's need to be free of guilt, you have probably been rewarded. If you enticed a person to share in a certain activity, the resulting benefit must have accrued to both of you. If you persuaded someone to play a game of tennis, you also participated in the sport.

Accordingly, whenever you sought to satisfy a psychological need in another person, the reward was shared, with benefits forthcoming for your own well-being. As you endeavored to help someone else meet his need for freedom from guilt, your own sense of guilt was diminished.

It is the old principle of giving in order to receive. A reciprocity is set in motion. A friend is considered a friend because of this mutual exchange of needs. By this time, if you have followed the general directions, even if only partially, each need satisfied in others has redounded to your advantage. You have cast bread upon the waters, and it was returned, enriching your own existence.

But, as an afterthought, let us ponder this emotion of guilt. Would we be better off if guilt were suddenly eliminated entirely?

Guilt, to the sociologist, is a tool for restraining primitive impulses which uncontrolled would make organized society impossible. Man, to survive, must have the cooperation of other human beings. The method devised by civilized people to assure such interdependence has been the implantation of guilt to prevent hacking to pieces a neighbor who has acted unjustly.

It would therefore seem obvious that we must encourage others to get rid of unreasonable guilt that interferes with mental health—while retaining those elements of guilt that are conducive to a better and saner society.

CHAPTER XII

Love Me

Ever since Eve emerged from Adam's rib, other myths have also continued to complicate relations between man and woman. More drivel has been written about love than of any other human emotion. Love has not only become the primary preoccupation of commercialism but has been made the tool of much fraud and exploitation of the unwary.

Love sells automobiles and chicken soup. And some would sell their grandmother's soul for the privilege of showing their rump in designer jeans. Songs of love put millions in the coffers of people who would hardly know the difference between that emotion and the feeling of a one-night stand in a sex escapade.

Yet in spite of the cynicism and the commercialism, love is possibly the most important psychological need of any person. Whether or not illusions are perpetuated by platitudes, it is still true that a person without love lacks a necessary nutrient for his mind and body—and for the inner recesses of his soul.

Corporate sales forces know the effectiveness of love as a lure and bait. He that is without love seeks to fill the void with material things. And the advertising world knows this all too well.

But the longing for substitutes for love seems real enough. Try to pick up a girl in a beat-up jalopy. A limousine? The salesman has his arguments. You can't buy love, so the cliché goes. However, the truth is that it is less comfortable making love in the back seat of a vintage car than in the luxury of a penthouse.

Do we mean that love can exist only in sumptuous surroundings, or that the opposite is true? Is a gold coin worth less in the pocket of a ragged suit than in the pocket of an expensive pair of pants?

Perhaps the sad fact is that money does make it easier to expand our contacts with the opposite sex because of the materialistic nature of our society. Love in a garret is therefore less likely to become everlasting bliss.

But up to now we have been talking not about love, but rather about the circumstances where it might occur. Once love is felt—in varying degrees—that is the gold coin. It is also true that it may soon slip from the vagabond's pocket or be enticed away to a Fifth Avenue mansion. Wherever it exists, it carries its own qualities of the gold coin.

Indeed there is scarcely a person in whom the germ of love cannot be discovered. But what is really love?

Love is the merging of oneself with another. It may seem selfish, since this absorption of another's personality into one's own leaves one the richer. But that richness is equally bestowed on both the lover and the loved one. It is therefore a means of meeting one's own need while at the same time meeting the need of someone else.

Before you attempt to help satisfy a client's need for love, you should be aware of the variety of means by which a person struggles to meet and satisfy that need. You can utilize some of these or others of your own choosing to help another person reach out for that happy state. Among these, you must learn to distinguish between infatuation and real love.

Infatuation is instant desire. It is often based only on the physical, one set of glands calling to another; or it may be based on material things, appearance and other temporary fancies. Although infatuation can progress to love, it is often like shifting sands, here today and gone tomorrow.

Love is a friendship that has finally caught on into a deeper relationship, having taken root and grown until it has blossomed into something more beautiful.

Infatuation is generally accompanied by insecurity. Although you are excited, missing is that calm acceptance of genuine happiness. Doubts arise with unanswered questions, little things that you'd rather not risk examining lest they mar your hopes of dreams come true.

Love, on the other hand, is mature acceptance of the lover's imperfections. In spite of this knowledge, you want him near you, knowing that he is yours.

Infatuation urges immediate possession. "We'll get married right away." The sexual attraction is often paramount; everything else somehow will become all right after we have bedded together. Infatuation is fraught with lack of confidence. Does he find someone else more attractive? Can I trust him? Could he be cheating with another girl?

Love, on the contrary, is a feeling of trust. You are elevated in self-worth, making you a better person. It develops slowly, more gradually than infatuation. But it is the gold coin. It will retain its value under adversity. Mutually you will confront the winds of change in the knowledge that both are strong enough to withstand the buffeting.

Having the determination to pull together, to adapt to new situations, is one of the important factors to strengthen a relationship. There should be a mutual commitment to withstand hardships and disappointments. A relationship cannot be expected to solve all physical, sexual, and social needs. But if it provides a means of satisfying the need to be loved, that is a key value of any relationship.

Thus love is cemented by companionship, sharing, and joy of being together. You, as the advocate of the Proxy Method, are committed to help your client in the fundamentals of sharing and trust.

Loneliness and the search for a mate affect both the underprivileged and the financially comfortable. Yet many people give less thought to choosing a mate than they do to buying a suit of clothes.

Our haste in selecting a love object is probably based on the vast sociological changes in our culture. The average American moves some fourteen times during his lifetime. Hometowns are left behind, as are family and friends. In past decades when a girl allowed herself to be an easy mark, the whole community knew about her promiscuity and the doubtfulness of her future fidelity. Without the familiarity the hometown provided, today's young people are really strangers when they mate.

How do people meet today? When a fellow sees an appealing girl at a party, he makes small talk, all the time wondering if she would go for intimacy. There are also entrepreneurs who arrange dances, clubs, even living quarters for mixed couples. Dating bureaus, some computerized, promise the ideal mate, the scientific way to love and fun.

Isolation of the sexes on campuses is gradually dying out. Even Princeton and Yale universities have gone co-ed. Dormitories allow males and females to share quarters. For some people living together is an easy way to gratify sexual needs, but many say that the arrangement is to avoid being lonely.

Many sociologists, however, predict that unless we find more effective ways of choosing mates, there will inevitably be an increase in troubled relationships. More unhappy people are seeking a more dependable method of satisfying their need for love.

Attracting the opposite sex is a game played since primordial times. It is still a fascinating and endless adventure. But attracting the opposite sex goes deeper than personal appearance. One has to make the best of what he has, and appearance is only one of the factors involved.

Suggest that your client jot down all his good points: his figure, a sense of humor, a frank and bright smile. Let him push out of his mind all that he considers to be his bad points, allowing him to concentrate on his positive aspects.

The person should keep in mind the desirability of making others feel comfortable. Compliments are always appreciated, making him someone pleasant to be with. He must be careful not to be a bore, monopolizing the conversation, talking too much about himself and his problems. Listening and taking an attentive interest in what the other person says is always flattering. He should show his appreciation for whatever is done on his behalf. Under no circumstances should he be critical. No one wants a date with one who is so uncivil as to make derogatory remarks about his companion. If your client makes what he considers to be a mistake, he should avoid profuse excuses, but rather make amends by doing something extra special for his date. In short, to be concerned with the other person within the limits of good taste is the essence of attracting the opposite sex.

With increasing pragmatism in our society, some people want the privilege of returning damaged or unsatisfactory goods—unsatisfactory partners—without the necessity of divorce or other complications. The arrangement is simple enough: a couple decide to live together to see if they are compatible. One woman stated without hesitation, "After all, I want to know how the man is in bed."

From a practical point of view, lack of sexual suitability is too often the real reason for divorce. Research has demonstrated that sexual problems are in the forefront in marital disharmony.

Apart from moral implications, it seems evident that such trial agreements might do what the participants claim. The question must be asked, however, whether the liaison is based on love or is merely a hedonistic device for less commendable purposes. Each person, as far as the social scientist is concerned, has the right to his own concept of right and wrong in matters of personal intimacy. And, of course, society has a claim when a wrong unfairly causes others to suffer.

But as one who is trying to help another person meet his need for love, you must not make judgments based on misconceived ideas in your value system. Your job under the Proxy Method is rather to encourage the means whereby the client can satisfy his need for a sense of loving and being loved in return.

Another unorthodox arrangement is the so-called open relationship in which partners engage in extramarital affairs. Mel Krantzler, author of *Creative Divorce*, describes open marriage as a "desperate maneuver" for people who don't know how to resolve their difficulties and fear the pursuit of more positive alternatives. He concludes that such a marriage is already dead; it destroys the basic trust necessary for a loving relationship.

If we are to equate openness and honesty with sleeping around, the marriage has little chance of continuing. Real love demands something special from someone special. What people really want is a committed relationship.

It is well for us to understand the sometimes self-defeating behavior of those who seek love, but we need not become reformers nor try to impose our own scale of values on others. But, in seeking to help others, we must recognize the rigid moralism and conformity that the inadequate person adopts because he cannot trust his own judgment.

Love comes in many forms with many varying objects. One

may love parents, brothers and sisters, and the boy next door. However, to assume that love is always a flaming torch from the heavens is to deny the more subdued relationships. Friendships are loves that few of us can do without. Although not making the demands of a lover, a friend frequently serves even better than a sexual liaison in satisfying the psychological need for love.

As an exponent of the Proxy Method, you may find it unfeasible to establish an intimate and physical relationship; however, you can become your client's friend in the true sense of the word.

You can accompany him to places where he will meet people—churches, singles bars, bowling alleys. You might also visit the same restaurant or bar regularly for coffee or a drink. Soon you and your client are accepted as regulars, a part of the ambience, recognized by employees and also by other customers who are considered regulars.

Once the circle of acquaintances has expanded, your own friendship for the client becomes a base from which he reaches for other friendships.

If in this process you are solely concerned with being a good friend, you will discover other ways to provide moral support and to make that person feel good. Trusting you gives your client a sense of security, a sense of being appreciated and loved.

In this process, it is necessary that you put aside your own needs for the time being. Here are guideposts for yourself:

Never show jealousy. Instead stress generous compliments.

Never display signs of envy. Show approval of the other's good points.

Never be boastful. Remember that you are now devoted to enhancing the other person's self-worth, not your own.

Never be haughty. The know-it-all attitude will be construed as arrogance or condescension.

Never be selfish. The rigidity of "What's in it for me?" is a real block to friendship. You can give in without coming unglued.

Never be rude. Love is always courteous. The greatest rudeness is the excuse of being too busy.

Never be irritable. Tension of that sort causes emotional and psychological problems.

Never hold a grudge. Keep looking ahead and forget the pain of the past.

Well, that's a list suitable for a saint, and the author has been guilty of platitudes. But the rules express a truth that is applicable in given situations with a definite purpose in mind—and remember you are not asking someone else to do these things; you are asked to use them as tools for a specific purpose. You will not, of course, be able to live up to all of them. But they can serve as a general guide, knowing that your primary aim is that of meeting another person's need for love and affection.

Overall, you have noted changes in another person as a result of your efforts to meet his need for love and affection. As the person joins hands with you, accepting your friendship, suddenly it is revealed that you yourself have acquired a real friend. By satisfying the need of someone else, you have automatically satisfied your own.

Having noted the variety of suggestions in this chapter, however, a lingering sense of ambiguity remains. And the truth is that the real essence of love has rarely been thoroughly examined.

What is this disturbing secret?

Unfortunately, love is not only sweetness and self-sacrifice. On the contrary, love is the most selfish of human emotions. When you love someone, you want to possess her entirely. No one else must share her intimacy. Until recently, a bride wore white to represent her virginity. We still have a need for the security obtained from another person's selfish love.

CHAPTER XIII

The Sex Need

The sex drive must find an outlet if one is to consider the total psychological needs of a person.

But sex is a bikini with a flimsy halter ever on the verge of slipping off. Sex may also be an ankle-length skirt and a blouse carefully fastened with a safety pin. Or sex is a billowing gingham dress with a pink scarf fluttering in a soft breeze. Or it may be subdued attire neat as a beautiful statue seemingly almost breathing with passion, but held back tantalizingly with simple allure.

Sex is what you make it, depending on your imagination, your character, your neurosis, or what you saw through a crack when you were five years old. It is the aura of angels, or the stink of an animal in heat. It can be the pedestrian joy of merely living, growing, and loving. Sex can provide the highest esctasies known to man or woman, or the agonies afflicting the lost.

Sex is hate and love. Sex is heaven and hell, disgust and the sweet scent of a delicate flower. The pervert drools over his pornography. The liberated goes from mate to mate still with the joy of sex largely denied. Another person contends that the sexual revolution is a myth, that sex is too precious to be taken lightly as a handshake or as an accommodation that goes with the motel furniture.

Regardless of accepted or rejected attitudes, it is noted that teenagers, for example, are increasingly active. According to a Public Health report, 41 percent of unmarried 17-year-old girls are having sexual intercourse. Half of teenage brides are already pregnant before marriage. It is estimated that these marriages have only one chance in ten of survival. Of course, one should take into consideration that on the average American girls begin to menstruate at about twelve and a half years of age. The sociological implications become clear when we realize that physical maturity occurred at seventeen years about a century ago.

With the increased promiscuity today, 33 percent of babies born to teenagers are illegitimate. Despite the opinion of mental health specialists that many of these young people are not ready for sex, they feel pressured by parents and society. If they do not embrace the new sexual freedom, they feel something must be wrong with them. Consequently one girl in sixteen becomes a mother by age seventeen. In addition to the high rate of divorces in that group, 9 percent of teenage mothers attempt suicide—seven times the rate for other teenagers.

Historically, boys had more sexual freedom than girls. But a recent survey indicates that the double standard is giving way to an individualistic ethic, an attitude that whatever a person feels is right and comfortable is permissible for both male and female.

The desire for sexual relations seems no longer a motivating factor for marriage. One common reason is the fear that the other person might engage in sex with someone else unless they settle down into matrimony.

For many, virginity is no longer a virtue. Experience with different sexual partners is assumed to be desirable in order to discover one's preference. Many young people view sexual experiences as an asset for a future committed relationship.

On the other hand, over 50 percent of teenagers questioned still felt that sex is very special, meant only for a permanent mate. They categorized anyone unmarried and sexually active as "loose," "promiscuous," or "a tramp."

Almost 90 percent of 25-year-olds in Great Britain favor sex before marriage, reports sociologist Michael Schofield in a survey for the Health Education Council. He says that young people should be encouraged to meet a large number of other young people before making any sexual commitment. Sex before marriage, he asserts, leads to many unsuitable marriages.

Of course, there are other pitfalls in sexual promiscuity. One of these is the possibility of venereal disease, now euphemistically termed STD for sexually transmitted disease. Until recently syphilis was considered most sinister because it could lead to insanity and death. Gonorrhea, in the past viewed as less serious than syphilis, has turned out to be more harmful. This is because some of the present strains of bacteria no longer respond to penicillin or tetracycline. Until a few years ago, another antibiotic called spectinomycin was effective against the resistant bacteria. Other antibiotics do work, but it is increasingly difficult to handle the disease.

Actually, there are a number of other ugly-looking forms of STD. Among them is the presently incurable scourge of genital herpes, now infecting over twenty million Americans.

Many myths are circulated about this ailment. It is believed, for example, that if you contract genital herpes, you'll soon know that you have it. The fact is that one can harbor and spread the virus and not be aware of it; often no symptoms are evident.

Another fallacy about genital herpes is that once you have it, you are doomed to lifetime flare-ups of the disease. The fact is that half of those who contract it are never bothered after the first outbreak.

It is said that if you haven't had herpes by the time you're thirty, you're probably immune. This notion is without foundation. One is vulnerable to this form of STD at any age, and indeed there is no proof that anyone is resistant to it.

It is also said that the disease can be transmitted only by sexual intercourse. The truth is that one can get it by kissing or by contact with any moist article in which the germ can survive for 72 hours.

The U.S. Food and Drug Administration has approved acyclovin for treatment of genital herpes, but the drug is not a cure. It has limited success in treating the initial outbreak of symptoms.

If there is no cure, one might assume that it is unnecessary to see a doctor; however, there are "look-alike" symptoms that are treatable.

Men and women are equally susceptible to herpes. The disease is not new, having been known for 2,000 years. What is unusual is that it has become epidemic in the U.S., with 300,000 to 500,000 new cases each year.

This fact is certainly serious enough to influence the many who tend to be promiscuous. But every person is free to take his chances, to do what he wants to do, provided he does not infringe on the rights of others. The tragedy is that so many people do not care how many others they infect. Those who knowingly pass on this scourge to others are angry persons who wish to punish others, projecting their self-hatred to people who trust them.

Apart from the dangers described, a discussion of sex may be interesting and instructive. Actual participation in sexual intercourse without love may be adventuresome, but it is generally little more satisfying than self-manipulation; the fulfillment is not there. The full esctasy of sex can be realized only through respect for the partner. Love is the magic elixir that transforms copulation into the most profound experience.

George Santayana, in 1902 writing of the future, said, "The masses of men will see no reason why they should not live out their native impulses or acquired passions without fear..." Unfortunately, Santayana did not foresee genital herpes. He might have been more encouraging if he could have predicted that the medical profession would be able to cure some of the results of "acquired passions."

The great English poet Shelley asked how a just God could create man with evil proclivities and then punish him for the weaknesses with which he endowed them. That, of course, is begging the question of each individual's self-responsibility. The bald fact is that each person has the right to go to hell if he so chooses.

But this decision may not be as conscious as one might conclude. When a teenager, for example, becomes sexually promiscuous, there are often underlying reasons. Many are not aware of the dynamics of their motivation. Some are trying to punish their parents for real or imagined wrongs. Dr. Rhoda Lorand, a psychologist, says that promiscuity in teenagers is always the result of emotional disturbance. When the home is disharmonious, without love or affection, the young person seeks to find some security in the arms of someone who at least values her body if not her heart and mind.

Parents who are overstrict and overprotective frequently

lead youngsters to use sex to break away from the emotional domination. "I can do anything I want to do," the girl exclaims in rebellion, seeking to establish her own identity. But sex used as a substitute for love at home is unrelated to tenderness and genuine affection. It tends to be less stimulating and generally unsatisfactory.

In ancient Greek and Hebrew, the verb "to know" meant to have sexual intercourse, as illustrated in the Bible: "Abraham knew his wife and she conceived ... "

The phrase "to know" today implies more than a passing acquaintance of infatuation. It means sharing thoughts and feelings as you try to encourage another person to relate to you in depth, revealing his true thoughts rather than superficial attitudes. In other words, a mating relationship should have a solid foundation in communication and knowledge of another. Sex cannot be isolated from caring and tender feelings based on trust and faith.

Unfortunately, many males have some very unreal ideas about sex. They are apt to withhold real sharing with a sex partner. They are impelled to appear other than what they are, and the resultant tension makes them less than forthright. Sex to such men is a performance that is being rated. They tend to think that all other men are having a better time sexually than they are. Being over-concerned with their partner's orgasm and their own instead of enjoying the process itself increases anxiety and deprives them of joy in what they are doing. Because of this myth that a man's performance is being judged, the entire meaning of sex is lost, and they cannot be honest and spontaneous in making love. They know neither themselves nor the object of their liaison.

Most men feel that they must take charge of the sexual act, that it is their right and responsibility to be aggressive. Of course, this male chauvinism robs the woman of the privilege of initiating the sexual act. The man, on the other hand, if he be secure in his masculinity, is denied the occasional enjoyment of passivity.

Further, all physical contacts and caresses are seen by the man as leading to the ultimate intimacy. If he would shed this attitude, he could not only lessen tension but also relish cuddling, hugging, and stroking without feeling that bed must be the immediate goal.

These and other false notions held by many men interfere with open and sincere physical contacts and, in fact, with most relations with the opposite sex.

Some people, on the other hand, are rebelling against this free-floating morality. They are revolting against the sexual revolution, charging that it is tearing apart the fabric of our country, creating all sorts of conflicts, destroying the family, and robbing young people of a sense of stability and security.

On one side are those who say that bigotry and prudery are the causes of neurosis and other mental illnesses. On the other side are those who assert that putting aside traditional values is the sign of a decadent society.

Clare Booth Luce, editor and former congresswoman, is alleged to have said, "What we call the New Morality is actually the old immorality of decadent civilizations." "Sexual permissiveness," says Col. Alex J. Stuart, president of the National Character Laboratory, "destroys a personal morality. We must return to the traditional American spirit of virtue and morality."

Dr. Paul Popenoe, family therapist, says, "The question of sexual permissiveness deeply affects our society, because bad sexual ethics are detrimental to the family..."

The national commander of the Salvation Army, William E. Chamberlain, says, "I believe free sex, infidelity and the 'anything goes' attitude of some people is unhealthy and antisocial. We must return to traditional standards of morality." Jack Hood Vaughn, president of Planned Parenthood of America and former director of the Peace Corps, says that "indiscriminate sex ruins thousands of lives each year." And the Rev. William McFadden, chairman of the theology department at Chicago University, expresses the opinion that "A marriage based on spiritual love will be much stronger than one built on sexual attraction."

In view of the wide differences of opinion in regard to sexual mores, some people stress the need for sex education in the schools in order to eradicate the vast ignorance of sexual matters.

For example, a survey of sex and birth control knowledge and practices among high school students revealed that 55 percent of the boys thought that no contraceptive was necessary if the girl used a douche. Half of the boys had their first sex experience at age thirteen. Girls thought that there was no chance of pregnancy in the first sexual act.

A more pragmatic approach is offered for early sex education as a means of reducing the number of mothers on welfare rolls. Prof. Donald J. Bogue of the University of Chicago asserts that the number of families on welfare could be reduced by 35 to 40 percent if an adequate sex education program were instituted in the schools.

There are also those who would recommend abstinence as the only sure way to avoid sexual problems, particularly in the unmarried. The fact remains that the sex urge cannot be entirely denied. Nevertheless, the more conservative exponents of greater control stress the necessity of sublimation of sex energy.

In sublimation, sexual energy is not cut off, but remains to be replaced by one that is no longer felt as sexual, funneled into acceptable courses. Sublimation of sex does not mean that sensuality is suspended. It is merely transmitted in another way.

The Greek philosopher Aristotle recognized art as a function of sublimation, stating that, "Emotions accumulated in us under stress of social restraint are apt to burst forth in unsocial and destructive action. Instead, these emotions are touched off and sluiced away in harmless form."

When one's sexuality is opposed without sublimation, it can give rise to neurotic symptoms, according to many modern psychologists. The sexual life of the person without healthy expression that minimizes frustration finds an outlet with considerable difficulty. Persistent frustration in the satisfaction of one's need frequently leads to the abandonment of desire for an object or a need. Women become frigid, unable to achieve orgasm, and men similarly develop dysfunctions such as impotence.

According to Sigmund Freud, sublimation may be the answer to the problem, since it consists in the diversion of the libidinal tendency from the original goal to a higher, socially valuable expression.

Up to now, we have surveyed a hodge-podge of opinions, views, and convictions in sexual matters. However, we have not forgotten that our primary aim in this chapter is to guide you, as a practitioner of the Proxy Method, to undertake the task of helping someone else to satisfy his sexual needs.

The first step in the procedure is therefore to study the issues discussed in this chapter and seek to determine where your client stands. Incidentally, ventilation of these issues with the person is in itself of value in satisfying sexual need.

If your client takes the hedonistic approach, you must not try to dissuade him from his view. If, on the other hand, it is one of abstinence, you will examine the justifications for such a position. In other words, if you are to help another person to meet his sexual need, you must be tolerant and open-minded, without prejudices.

However, there are areas of common benefit for the person who is sexually active. And the principles that you can discuss without being dogmatic are as follows.

The sex act is most satisfying if both participants can abandon themselves wholly to the pleasure. This involves a selfishness in the sense that the mate, feeling the full self-absorption of the lover, responds with an intensity of his own.

There should be a sense of security, without any doubts or lack of sincerity in the other person. This also involves open and frank communication, brushing aside any guilt or shame.

One should never criticize in any sexual situation. Anything negative lessens the man's potency as well as the woman's excitement. The atmosphere surrounding the sex act should be one of relaxation, without the lowering of self-worth.

Loving should not be a hurried affair. People who are sure of their sexual power take time to caress, kiss, and engage in other foreplay that intensifies desire and arouses greater excitement and satisfaction.

Praise and evident respect for one's mate enhance the experience and the feeling of security. The relationship should be nondemanding and considerate of the other's state of passion and desire, thus providing the most favorable climate for the fulfillment of one's sexual need.

As the exponent of the Proxy Method, it now becomes evident that in helping someone else to meet his sexual need, you have gone through a process whereby you have become more conscious of your own need and how to satisfy it. Again, by helping another person, you have received a rich reward, which, even if it had not been anticipated, still redounds to your own benefit, self-understanding, and growth.

In past ages, plagues periodically swept over the world; the cities counted their dead while those still alive anticipated their own early journey to the grave. Only recently in modern history has the medical profession seemed to deliver us from such catastrophes. And yet as we proclaimed a sexual revolution, a new predator came upon us like a fierce animal on padded feet in the night. And suddenly we peered deeper in the beast's eyes and there saw AIDS—the equivalent of a death sentence. People knew not whom to blame except minorities until at last we realized that actually we were all guilty.

No one can escape the problem, since it concerns society as a whole. All sexual expression must now confront the threat of AIDS like a shroud casting a dark shadow over our sex lives.

CHAPTER XIV

Recapitulation

Suppose, for illustrative purposes, that you felt without a sense of belonging, without friends, lover, or even relatives. And further suppose that you were without any sense of achievement, denied talents or skills, or the opportunity to do anything considered significant by others. Add to that a feeling of inadequacy exacerbated by feelings of fear and guilt. Finally your love and sex life are troublesome, filled with conflicts and denied any outlets.

Certainly that would be a sad state of affairs. And you will readily agree that with all those denials and deprivations, you would be far from happy—and probably one to be pitied in the darkness of your soul. You would be beset by frustrations too severe to bear.

The first principle of the Proxy Method is therefore that frustrations are the culprits in causing many emotional disorders, including loneliness. Much research has been conducted by scientists in the past decade to prove that frustrations do cause self-defeating behavior and neurotic dysfunctions. However, merely considering the above suppositions convinces you that frustration of psychological needs never leads to happiness or freedom from emotional upsets.

But you may say, "If it's just the simple matter of satisfying my needs, why can't I do that through my own determination and willpower?" Some few people do exactly that, but the person plagued with chronic loneliness obviously hasn't been able to handle his own problem. Accordingly, he requires a better method to get rid of his alienation in order to offset his tendency to shy away from the problem.

How many New Year's resolutions have you made—and how many have you kept? Somehow there is in each of us a tendency to defeat ourselves—a force inclining us to destructive action or inaction. This is opposed by a force for success and constructive behavior. Freud talked of these two instincts. He called one the death instinct, existing side by side with the life instinct—respectively known as *thanatos* and *eros.*

Whether or not we agree with Freud, the fact still remains that at times it is difficult for us to stick to a course that obviously is for our benefit. The lonely person is already caught in a mesh of discouragement; it is hard for him by willpower alone to extricate himself from bad habits.

However, you do not need statistical analysis by social scientists to prove that you must have some vital satisfaction and recognition for your existence. The first principle of the Proxy Method is therefore self-evident as judged from your everyday experiences. You are comparatively happy when you possess a sense of belonging, the satisfaction of achievement, whether it be on the football field or knitting a pair of sox. And certainly you have no need to be told that to be rid of fears and guilt is good for you. As for love and sexual adjustment, these are obviously of importance for your peace of mind.

The first equation is therefore:

Frustration=Trouble

The second principle of the Proxy Method follows logically: if frustrations are caused by unmet needs, then satisfying those needs will eliminate the frustrations.

The second equation is therefore:

Met needs=Removal of frustration

The third principle of the Proxy Method is implied in its name. It is a way of providing a workable procedure to satisfy a person's psychological needs. The method has achieved considerable success in psychotherapy.

The Proxy Method gets around the tendency to avoid positive action purely for a selfish reason. Instead of working for yourself, you let others do the job. In other words, you forget about yourself and your problem, the fact that your own psychological needs have been denied. Instead of working for yourself, you devote your time to others.

In doing that, you help others to meet their needs. In the process you lose self-centeredness and forget your own loneliness. And as if by magic you discover that you no longer have a problem. You help yourself merely by helping others.

In a study, Dr. Bernard Rimland, director of the Institute for Child Behavior Research, discovered that selfish people, those who won't go out of their way to help others, tend to be unhappy, and those of opposite inclinations tend to be happy. Thus we can draw a surprising conclusion that one way to be selfish is to be unselfish. The golden rule, do unto others as you would have them do unto you, is not necessarily altruistic; actually it has the element of its opposite nature.

The third equation is therefore:

Unselfishness=Selfishness

Lest you conclude that our three equations are somewhat ruthless and a rather cynical game, rest assured that they have solid foundation in Judeo-Christian morality. The fact that you derive so much benefit from the Proxy Method does not detract from the fact that you help others in the process.

The procedures described for fulfilling the needs of others do not have to be systematized. You can choose several persons or only one individual, and you need not follow the order given in the preceding chapters. Nor are you required to meet all the needs—each one is of value in itself. You merely spread "the sunshine" wherever the opportunity warrants. What really counts is the total effect on you.

This program will engender amazing changes, making you a different person, a lovable personality, with loneliness only a vague memory of the past before you discovered the secret of self-fulfillment, peace of mind, and self-confidence. The formula of the Proxy Method is as old as the prophets, philosophers, and religious leaders of past centuries. Imbibe their wisdom, find a new identity, and a happier you.

Index

abstinence, 111-112
accident proneness, 41-42
achievement, need for, 73-79, 81, 115
AIDS (acquired immunodeficiency
 syndrome), 113
alcohol abuse, 20, 29
amphetamines, 49
anger, 12, 37, 40, 83, 92
 and lonelinesss, 17-26
 repression of, 68, 91
anorexia nervosa, 42, 45
anxiety, 17, 24, 27, 33, 40, 73, 83, 91
 and loneliness, 11-15
automobile, as weapon, 39-40

barbiturates, 52-53
behavior
 antisocial, 6
 irrational, 93
 self-defeating, 3, 46, 101
 unacceptable, 26
 unreasonable, 4
belonging, sense of, 65, 68, 115
breasts, as sex symbols, 32

cocaine, 51
codeine, 49
communication, 67, 84
cosmic loneliness, 4
cultural loneliness, 4

death instinct, 37-38, 116
drug abuse, 5, 47-59

failure, fear of, 11, 78
fears, 115
 irrational, 15
 lessening, 83-89
friendship, 69-70, 71, 98, 102
frustration, 9, 17, 18, 30, 33, 40, 68, 83,
 91, 111, 115, 116

guilt, 14, 17, 33, 37, 83, 87, 115
 lessening, 91-95

hallucinogens, 53-59
heroin, 6, 48-49

infatuation, 98-99
interpersonal loneliness, 4

life instinct, 38, 116
listening, importance of, 75, 94
love, need for, 44, 85, 97-103
LSD, 55-56

marijuana, 54-55
mental illness, 42, 110
morphine, 48

needs, psychological
 denial of, 17, 33, 39, 47-48, 87, 92
 meeting of, 11, 66, 75, 79, 92, 97-98,
  102, 115, 116
 unmet, 9, 12, 14, 37, 73, 76

opium, 47-48

penis
 envy, 33
 size of, 31
permissiveness, sexual, 110
phobia, 23-24, 84-86
promiscuity, 106, 108
Proxy Method, 63-64, 71-72, 80, 85, 88-
 89, 99, 101, 112, 115, 117

rejection, fear of, 3, 5, 24, 28, 37, 68, 74,
 83
relationship
 family, 18-19
 interpersonal, 14, 27
 love, 31, 99-102, 106
 love-hate, 42